The Little iTunes Book

Second Edition

Bob LeVitus

Peachpit Press • Berkeley, California

The Little iTunes Book, Second Edition
Bob LeVitus

Peachpit Press
1249 Eighth Street
Berkeley, CA 94710
510/524-2178
800/283-9444
510/524-2221 (fax)

Find us on the World Wide Web at: www.peachpit.com
To report errors, please send a note to errata@peachpit.com
Peachpit Press is a division of Pearson Education

Copyright 2003 by Bob LeVitus

Editor: Kate McKinley
Production Coordinator: Lisa Brazieal
Compositor: Diana Van Winkle
Indexer: Karin Arrigoni
Cover Design: John Tollett and Mimi Heft
Cover Illustration: Trish Booth

ISBN 0-321-16886-0

9 8 7 6 5 4 3 2

Printed and bound in the United States of America

For Jacob and Allison:
You're not just my favorite movie subjects,
you're my two favorite kids in the whole entire world.
Love,
Daddy

Acknowledgements

First and foremost: Thank you for buying my book.

This book was a team effort. Though my name appears on the cover, it wouldn't exist without the extraordinary efforts of that team. And so, before we go any further, I'd like to take this opportunity to express my heartfelt gratitude to all of them...

Major thanks to Peachpit Press Publisher (try saying that three times fast) Nancy Ruenzel and Executive Editor Marjorie Baer, for believing in this project and giving it the green light.

Big time thanks to Lisa Brazieal, production coordinator extraordinaire, for keeping the whole affair on track week in and week out, and to awesome freelance editor Kate McKinley, who not only minded my Ps and Qs, but managed to keep the word "stuff" from appearing on every page. I'd also like to thank Diana Van Winkle, for composing these gorgeous pages in record time.

My super duper literary agent, Carole McClendon at Waterside Productions, deserves praise for stellar deal-making on my behalf, year in and year out. I'm still gonna call her "Swifty," though.

And my wife, Lisa, and my kids, Allison and Jacob, have certainly earned very special thanks for putting up with my all-too-frequent hibernations, and giving me the space to do what I do. I love you guys all the muches.

I'm almost done...but I'd be remiss if I didn't also thank Apple—both for creating iTunes and pricing it right.

And last, but certainly not least, very special thanks to Senior Technical Editor, Victor Gavenda, for excellent technical observations and insights too numerous to count (not to mention his extremely humorous editorial comments).

Table of Contents

Chapter 8 Music on the Internet   121

Chapter 9 Internet Radio   135

PART FOUR: MORE STUFF YOU SHOULD PROBABLY KNOW

Chapter 10 Compression and Sound Quality   145

Introduction

I love iTunes. I've loved it from the moment I first saw it. I even remember precisely when that moment was—almost two years ago now, on January 9, 2001, at 10 A.M., during Steve Jobs's keynote address at Macworld Expo in San Francisco.

As usual, we (the audience) had no idea what rabbits Jobs was going to pull out of his hat. He made a slew of wonderful new-product announcements, including iDVD, the PowerBook G4 Titanium, the first recording CD drives in Macs, and a ship date for Mac OS X. But what knocked my socks off was iTunes.

You see, I'm a music lover and always have been. I listen to music constantly—at my desk, in my car, in my bedroom, and at the gym. I'm listening to Elvis—playing in iTunes, of course—as I type. So it should come as no surprise that I was an early adopter of MP3 technology, downloading every freeware, shareware, or demoware MP3 player that came along, looking for one that worked the way I wanted it to.

My early efforts at using MP3s and creating audio CDs were fraught with frustration, however. The software was buggy, the encoders were slow, and the software took over my Mac completely (ah, the joys of Mac OS 9), not allowing me to work while I burned a CD. (Don't be alarmed if you don't know what all of that means— I promise that when you finish reading this book, you'll even be able to explain it to other people.) Furthermore, burning audio CDs from MP3 files was always a chancy proposition, just as likely to produce a drink coaster as a music CD that I could listen to in the car or on my portable CD player.

We've come a long way since then, gentle reader. Today, we can do all that and more, quickly, easily, and reliably, with iTunes 3—the latest, greatest version of iTunes yet.

The Dad Test

One day (pre-iTunes) when I was visiting my father, an avid but rather unsophisticated iMac user, I played one of my home-made CDs for him. He loved the concept. He asked if I could show him how to do that. I thought back on all the trouble I'd had getting my setup working, the multistep process, and the two separate programs and several system extensions he'd have to install. I also thought about the cost of the software and hardware. And I was forced to reply, "I'm afraid not."

Then I saw version 1 of iTunes, a single, elegant program that managed your music collection effortlessly, ripped songs from CD to hard disk quickly and easily, burned custom audio CDs painlessly (and without taking over your Mac), and displayed some of the coolest visual effects I've ever seen. It was the first MP3 rip-and-burn program to pass my "Dad test" with flying colors: I could teach Dad enough about it in half an hour to have him burning custom CDs to his heart's content.

But I realized that although I could teach him enough about iTunes in half an hour to burn a CD, it would take me a lot longer to explain everything he'd need to know to burn *great-sounding* CDs. Under ordinary circumstances, I'd say, "Read the fine manual," and that would be the end of it. But iTunes has never come with any type of printed manual. The best it can offer is the stuff you'll find in its Help menu.

It was obvious that what was needed was a short, entertaining, yet comprehensive, guide to using iTunes, written in a style Dad would easily understand. And that, gentle reader, is how the first edition of *The Little iTunes Book* came to be.

About This, the Second Edition

The first edition of this book proved me right—I'm pleased to report that it has sold beyond our wildest expectations. (Thank *you* for that!) But with the introduction of the iPod and iTunes 3, the first edition had become badly outdated.

Fortunately, the nice folks at Peachpit Press asked me to give the whole book an overhaul and update. So every nook and cranny has been reinspected; every word and picture rescrutinized; every bad joke, worse pun, and obscure musical reference reviewed; and every mistake I know of repaired.

Furthermore, every new feature in iTunes 3 is covered in full and loving detail—Smart Playlists; content from Audible.com; the Sound Check volume normalizer; star ratings; the Play Count, Last Played, and Composer fields; joining separate tracks on import; and sharing playlists, to name a few.

Who Should Read This Book

Everyone should read this book, of course, even people who use Windows computers. (My accountant made me say that— iTunes is, of course, a Mac-only program.)

All kidding aside, this book is for anyone and everyone who uses iTunes. More specifically, it's for people who want to know more about the program, and about making CDs, than they'll find in the iTunes Help system. But most of all, it's for iTunes users who want to learn how to burn great-sounding audio CDs.

I make very few assumptions in this book, but I do assume that you know the basics of using Mac OS X (iTunes 3 is OS X–only), such as how to launch a program, insert a CD, click, double-click, use menus, create folders, and so on. If you're fuzzy on any of those concepts, I recommend you read one of Robin Williams's books for beginners—*The Little Mac Book, The Little iMac Book*, or *The Little iBook Book*—before you dig into this one.

Robin is my favorite Mac writer. Frankly, I like her writing better than I like my own! Her Little Books are gems, and they're my inspiration for this book—easy to read and understand, yet filled with tips, tricks, hints, and techniques that will have even brand-new Mac users up to speed in just a few hours.

One Last Thing

The world of digital audio uses some specialized terms (such as *MP3* and *bit rate*), as well as some ordinary words (such as *burn* and *rip*) with specialized meanings. Rather then stick the definitions in a Glossary at the end of the book where you'll never see it, I've included a definition of each term on the same page where I first use it. If you forget a term, you can always check the Index to find that definition. I also use several icons to highlight parts of the text.

The Note icon tells you that the accompanying text is not essential, though it's interesting or useful.

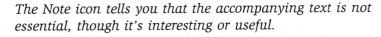

The Tip icon tells you that the accompanying text contains an important time-saving tip or trick that it would be helpful to learn.

The Warning icon is only used when what I'm saying is so important that ignoring it could have disastrous consequences. I don't use warning icons often in this book, so if you see one, read carefully.

All righty, then. Let's move along to the fun stuff.

P.S. While I can't promise to answer every email message I receive, I do answer as many as I can. If you have a comment or a question about something I've written, please feel free to send me an email; I usually answer them within a day or two. My email address is *LITB2E@boblevitus.com.*

Which reminds me: I'd like to thank everyone who bought a copy of the first edition of this book, and especially the readers who sent emails, asked questions, shared their observations and suggestions, and even wrote me "thank you" notes. I've done my best to answer your questions and integrate your suggestions in this edition.

P.P.S. If you're curious, the address is an acronym for *Little iTunes Book 2nd Edition.* Using this address (as opposed to my usual one, boblevitus@boblevitus.com) gives it a better chance of making it past my numerous and extremely aggressive anti-spam filters.

part
one
Getting to Know iTunes

In the Beginning

Describing iTunes reminds me of the old story about the blind men describing an elephant, in which each man feels a different part of the animal, then disagrees with his fellows' descriptions. Similarly, one user might say that iTunes is a program that converts songs on audio CDs into smaller and more convenient MP3 files. Another might describe iTunes as the perfect program to categorize, organize, and search through a lot of MP3 files quickly and easily. A third might tell you that iTunes is a CD burner that lets you create your own custom CDs quickly and easily. And a fourth might declare that iTunes is the world's most elegant and easy-to-use MP3 player.

And, just like with the elephant, everyone is right: iTunes is an MP3 encoder, a music organizer, an MP3 player, and a CD burner (and much more, as you'll see in upcoming chapters), all wrapped up in a single program.

Before I show you how to use iTunes, I'd like to provide a brief lesson on the history of digital sound, MP3, and the Macintosh. The way I see it, you'll understand what you're doing much better if you understand a bit about the underlying technology. I promise to keep it short, sweet, and relatively painless.

The (Extremely Abridged) History of Sound and the Mac

Before the Macintosh, sound on personal computers was positively primitive. Although some personal computers could beep and boop, none of them could talk, play music, or record sounds. In fact, before the Mac, a computer that could do such things was more or less unthinkable. Then in 1984, the Mac came along and the unthinkable became commonplace.

Picture this, if you will: The date is January 24, 1984. The place is the annual Apple shareholders meeting at Flint Center in Cupertino, California. The Mac has never been shown publicly before today. Steve Jobs walks onto the stage carrying a plain canvas sack. He pulls out a Mac, places it on a table, and says, "I'd like to let the Macintosh speak for itself." The Mac replies, in that goofy mechanical voice, "Hello, I am Macintosh. It sure is great to get out of that bag."

Over the years there have been other audio-related firsts for the Mac. For example, the Mac was the first computer to include software that let you listen to music CDs while you worked. The Mac was also the first computer to include a microphone, and software to use it with. Though some expensive, single-purpose computers did it first, the Mac was the first popularly priced computer to offer multitrack music recording.

MPEG stands for Moving Pictures Experts Group. These are the folks who developed many popular compression systems used for video today, which are collectively known as MPEG in their honor.

MP3 is one subset of MPEG compression, used exclusively to compress sound. Its full name is MPEG audio layer 3, so you can understand why almost everyone refers to it by its acronym, "MP3." MP3 is the compression system used by iTunes and most other computer audio player/encoders. MP3 reduces the file size of a song from a prerecorded CD without hurting the quality of what you hear (much).

Burn is another way to say "record" when you're talking about making your own CDs. Here's how to use it in conversation: "I'm going to burn a CD later" or "I'm burning a CD now." While this usage might alarm the fire marshall, everyone else will think you're way cool.

Encode means to convert a file from one format to another. (Another word for this is *rip*. As in, "I ripped a bunch of songs today.") For example, when you use iTunes to convert an AIFF file into a smaller MP3 file, you're said to be encoding that file.

Compression and MP3

The MP3 format began its meteoric rise to popularity in the mid-1990s. MP3 is a compression system that reduces the size of audio files by up to 90 percent without affecting the way they sound (or at least not much). You see, the tracks on an audio CD are huge digital files in a format called "Red Book" (yes, there actually is a red book), or "CD-DA."

Savvy computer users would convert songs on CDs into computer files (MP3s) that were much smaller than the original but still sounded good (see **Figure 1.1**). That way, they could keep lots of songs on their hard disks, email songs to other MP3 users, and fit an entire song on a floppy disk.

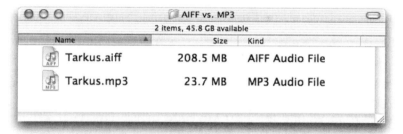

Figure 1.1 Encoding the AIFF file (a Red Book or CD-DA audio file; top) yields an MP3 file about one-tenth the size (bottom).

Most MP3 files sport the .mp3 suffix for easy identification.

Compression is the act of encoding data files so they take up less storage space. The amount a file can be compressed depends entirely on the type of file and the compression method used. MP3 compression can often reduce a file's size to a tenth or less.

AIFF stands for audio interchange file format. AIFF files allow the storage of sounds (usually music) on Macintosh disks in an uncompressed form. The Windows equivalent of AIFF is the WAV format. Since AIFF and WAV files are not compressed in any way, they are much larger than compressed audio files such as MP3 files. As a rule of thumb, 1 minute of music in AIFF or WAV uses about 10 MB of disk space.

CD-DA or "Red Book" is a technical specification for audio CDs that provides essential details—such as sampling and transfer rates—to ensure that the songs on that CD can be played by any CD player.

Unless you have very sensitive ears, you probably won't be able to tell the difference between the MP3 version of a song and the much larger version on the original CD. Even the most avid audiophile would be hard pressed to discern a large AIFF song from a small MP3 song on most computer speakers or car stereos (even very good ones). You'll find out a lot more about compression and sound quality, and precisely what to listen for, in Chapter 10.

But the software they used to encode AIFF files into MP3 files, as well as the software they used to play MP3 files (often two different programs), was hard to find and not particularly easy to use if you found it. Furthermore, it was almost all shareware or freeware, with minimal documentation and customer support. So for a while, MP3 was growing in popularity, but primarily among devoted music lovers and computer enthusiasts.

Then in the late '90s, two factors converged that helped propel MP3 into the mainstream.

First, hard disks had grown to gargantuan proportions while plummeting in price. (For example, way back in 1987 I paid more than $2,000 for a 20 MB hard drive. This year I bought a 60 GB hard drive for under $300.) So computer users had tons of extra disk space, which many of them used for their collections of MP3 music files.

Shareware is software distributed for a nominal fee (freeware, obviously, requires no fee at all). The tradeoff is that there is no guarantee the software will work, and it usually has little or no documentation and customer support.

CD-R stands for compact disc–recordable. A CD-R drive is a device that can create (or burn) both CD-ROMs that can be used with most CD-ROM drives and audio CDs that can be played in most consumer audio CD players. (CD-ROM, by the way, stands for CD–read-only memory, and refers to any pre-recorded disc.) CD-R drives use inexpensive blank CD-R discs, which usually cost 50 cents or less each. Once you've recorded a CD-R, that's the end of it—the disc is "frozen." You can't add more data or music, nor can you erase and re-record the disc.

Any Mac with a CD-ROM drive can read data discs (CDs with Mac files on them) burned with a CD-R drive. With special software (such as Toast, which is included with many CD-R drives), you can also create CD-ROM data discs that Windows PCs can read.

Second, many PC manufacturers (though not Apple—yet) began to offer CD recorders (generally CD-R drives) built right into their computers, and included free MP3 player/encoder programs on the hard disk.

In addition to recording, CD-R drives can read both CD-ROM discs and audio CDs, just like an ordinary CD-ROM drive. So you don't have to have both a CD-R and a CD-ROM drive (though some people do have both).

By 1999, MP3 had moved into the mainstream. Any decent software store carried several different commercial MP3 player programs for your Mac (or other PC), and the dozens of share-ware and freeware programs had, not surprisingly, become easier to use. You could also buy inexpensive portable MP3 players, so you could take your tunes with you wherever you went.

And by the year 2000, you could buy a Windows PC that came with everything you'd need to encode MP3 files, listen to them on your computer, and create your own CDs.

There Are CD-DAs and There Are MP3-CDs

If you burn a data CD full of MP3 files, it's a data CD full of computer files. Macs (and possibly PCs, depending on the disc format you specified when you burned it) will be able to read it, but many older audio CD players will not. To create an audio CD that plays in any audio CD player, you burn the CD in CD-DA format. (As you'll see a few chapters hence, iTunes does this for you, automatically converting your MP3 files into CD-DA when you burn an audio CD.)

It should be noted that many audio CD players these days (including at least one from Sony) can play a data CD full of MP3 files. This is a way-cool feature—it lets you put hundreds of songs on a single CD. In the first edition of this book I said, "Unfortunately, this type of audio CD player—sometimes referred to as a 'CD/MP3 combo player'—is still relatively rare and somewhat more expensive than a plain old audio CD player."

I'm pleased to report that is no longer the case. Today you can buy this type of player at almost any store that sells inexpensive electronic devices—BestBuy, Circuit City, Fry's, and even Target and K-Mart—at prices starting under $50.

iTunes at Last

It wasn't until January 2001 that Apple began shipping an MP3 player/encoder on every Mac (that's iTunes, of course), and offering built-in CD-RW drives. And though Apple wasn't the first to do it, it was the first to do it right, and it was the first to make the whole MP3 experience easy enough for Dad, as well as good enough for me—and it's fun, too.

Before I forget: CD-RW discs are not compatible with most audio CD players. Unless yours specifically states it's capable of playing CD-RW discs, don't do it.

All Macs these days come with an optical disc burner of some type—a CD-R/CD-RW burner at the very least. The next step up is a "combo drive" that offers DVD playback (but not burning) combined with CD-R/CD-RW burning. But the top-of-the-line Apple SuperDrive (made by Pioneer) is the best deal of all—it can read and write more than a dozen different optical disc formats including DVD, DVD-R, DVD-RW, VideoCD, CD-ROM, CD-DA, CD-R, and CD-RW. For less than $5 you can burn a 4.7 GB DVD-R (or, for a few bucks more, a reusable DVD-RW) any time your hard disk starts getting too full. Aside from costing more than other optical drives, the only downside to the SuperDrive is that it reads and writes CD-R and CD-RW discs much slower than its dedicated CD-burning brethren.

Before iTunes, you could, of course, encode and listen to MP3s on a Mac. And you could burn your own audio CDs with third-party software such as Toast or Jam and an external CD recorder. But since the process involved hardware and software from several different vendors, you were frequently on your own if you encountered a problem. One vendor would blame the other for what went wrong, and getting a straight answer could be a challenge.

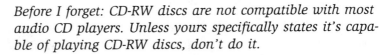

DVD stands for digital versatile disc (or digital video disc, depending on whom you ask). In addition to being a big, cheap storage medium (DVDs can hold 4.7 GB of data), DVD is becoming the standard for digital media—mostly because it's the first cosumer medium to offer interactivity that isn't tied to a computer or Web connection.

iTunes changes all of that. Apple is the first (and only) computer maker that "owns" the entire process from start to finish. It makes the computer, the operating system, the CD-RW drive, and the iTunes software—and it ensures that all the pieces work together, so that encoding MP3 files, organizing your music collection, and burning CDs is easier than ever. No other computer vendor or operating system maker can say the same.

Apple doesn't actually manufacture its own CD-RW drives, but the CD-RW drives built into Macs are considered "Apple branded," which means they are sold, serviced, guaranteed, and certified to work flawlessly with iTunes, by Apple.

Furthermore, if you have a problem with any part of the process, you can make a single call for support—to Apple. And Apple won't blame another vendor (though support *can* be spotty at times).

A Brief Look at Some of What iTunes Does

As I said at the beginning of this chapter, iTunes is an MP3 encoder, a music organizer, an MP3 player, and a CD burner, among other things. You can use it to encode CD-DA files into any of three file formats: AIFF, MP3, and WAV. You can also encode an AIFF file, turning it into an MP3 or WAV file. You can encode a WAV file into an AIFF or MP3 file. You can encode an MP3 file into an AIFF or WAV file. And you can encode any of the three formats into CD-DA.

Though the actual file formats are different (because AIFF is a Mac file format and WAV is a Windows file format), iTunes deals with AIFF and WAV files in exactly the same way. So if you somehow end up with a WAV file on your Mac hard disk— if a Windows user emails you a WAV file or you download one from the Web—iTunes can encode it into a smaller MP3 file as easily as it encodes an AIFF file.

I'd be remiss if I didn't mention that there are two kinds of compression—lossless and lossy. When you compress a word processing file or a spreadsheet or other similar types of files, the compressed file must contain exactly the same information as the original file, without losing a single bit of data. This is "lossless compression." StuffIt (.sit files) on the Mac and Zip (.zip files) in Windows are lossless compression formats.

By the way, don't bother trying to compress an MP3 file with a compression program such as StuffIt. Because MP3 files are already compressed, they won't get smaller if you compress them again.

But audio (and video) files can often be compressed to as little as 5 percent of their original size, using "lossy compression." This means the compressed files do not contain exactly the same information as the original. In fact, some of the data in the original file is lost when you compress it, but the loss is (usually) not noticeable to the human ear or eye. MP3 and MPEG are "lossy" compression formats.

How does MP3 work its magic? By "throwing away" parts of the sound spectrum that are mostly masked by other parts of the spectrum, and throwing away parts of the sound that our ears can't discern. The end result is a much smaller file that sounds almost as good as the original.

Speaking of losing things, you might think that with the smaller file sizes, you'll have more music on your hard disk and won't be able to find the song you want, when you want it. Not so: iTunes keeps track of your MP3s for you. Even if you can only remember part of a song title or an artist's name, iTunes can help you track it down, with a handy Search feature. And iTunes lets you group songs into "playlists," so you can make up your own perfect mood music. And the latest, greatest version, iTunes 3, will even offer to organize your iTunes Music folder, intelligently grouping your song files by artist and by album.

We'll take a closer look at all these topics in upcoming chapters, but I did want you to get a taste here in Chapter Numero Uno.

As for burning your own CDs—well let's take a look at what you'll need to get started.

Before Using Tunes 2

If you're new to iTunes, this chapter will give you an overview of what you need to get started. Not to mention some things you don't really need, but may want.

If you're a veteran iTunes user, you probably have everything I talk about in the first section, "Mandatory Stuff." Still, you might want to read it anyway, so you don't miss the feeble jokes, obscure musical references, and occasional bad puns. Everyone should definitely read the second section, "Optional Stuff," because it's chock-full of useful information about things you may or may not have already. And of course you don't want to risk missing all those feeble jokes, obscure musical references, and bad puns.

Mandatory Stuff

There are only four things you absolutely need to use iTunes: an appropriate Macintosh, the iTunes software, lots of disk space (to store your MP3 library), and a love of music. All right, you don't really need a love of music. But it helps. The rest you really do need.

A Mac

To use iTunes, you need a Macintosh computer. But not just any old Mac will do—iTunes is only supported on Macs with built-in USB ports. All iMacs, eMacs, iBooks, and G4s have 'em, as do most (but not all) desktop and PowerBook G3 models. Alas, older Macs with first-generation PowerPC chips (such as the PowerPC 601, 603, and 604) are not supported.

When Apple says other models aren't supported, it doesn't mean that iTunes won't work on them, it just means don't come crying to Apple for help. In fact, iTunes works just fine on many older Mac models, even some that lack such modern frippery as USB ports.

Almost all USB devices, including most keyboards, offer one or more "extra" USB ports for your convenience.

The iTunes program

Where can you get iTunes? Well, if your Mac has a built-in CD-RW, combo, or SuperDrive optical drive, iTunes came pre-installed on your hard disk. And even if you don't have a copy, you can download one (free) from www.apple.com/itunes.

iTunes 3 requires Mac OS X (10.1.4 or later). If you're using OS 9.0.4 or later, you can use iTunes 2 to rip and listen to MP3s, but to burn CDs you'll need Mac OS 9.1 or later.

The pitchfork-looking thing on this USB port (left) and USB connector (right) is the USB logo.

USB stands for universal serial bus (a "bus" is a pathway for data). USB technology is used to connect devices to your Mac that don't require superfast access, such as keyboards, mice, hard disks, digital cameras, and portable MP3 players. All Macs introduced since 1999 have at least one USB port.

Interestingly, in the first edition of the book I said, "Windows users are completely out of luck. I can't imagine Apple ever releasing a version of iTunes for Windows." And while that's still true, Apple has done the heretofore unthinkable and released iPods for Windows. Of course, Windows users are stuck with the inferior MusicMatch Jukebox software, but hey, at least they have the 'Pods now. Many of us didn't think even that would happen. As Apple shareholders will tell you, money talks, bullstuff walks, and those Windows iPods are flying off the shelves!

Plenty of disk space

Though disk space requirements for iTunes are modest (about 20 MB of space on your hard drive), the more you use iTunes, the more space you'll need on your hard disk (or other disk) for your MP3 files. A good rule of thumb is to allow 2 MB to 4 MB of disk space per song, though your mileage may vary.

For example, in this book's first edition I said I had 525 MP3s that used 2.36 GB of space on my hard disk; today I have more than 1,300 songs in my iTunes Music folder, which take up 5.8 GB. Put another way, the average song on my hard disk uses about 4.5 MB of disk space. As it did before.

If you're math impaired (like me—I had to ask my wife about it), here's how that works: 2.36 GB divided by 525 songs equals a little more than 4.49 MB per song. Interestingly, while I now have more than twice as many songs, the average song length has not changed much—5.8 GB divided by 1,300 songs equals 4.4 MB per song!

Size Matters!

Your average song will probably be smaller than mine. Why? Because I have a lot of very long songs in my collection, such as Emerson, Lake, and Palmer's "Tarkus," Iron Butterfly's "In-A-Gadda-Da-Vida," and Neil Young's "Like a Hurricane," each of which runs 10 to 20 minutes. Plus, I have a bunch of live bootleg recordings (sssh, don't tell the artists) that are that long or longer. Long songs, as you'd expect, take up more disk space than short ones.

The point is, you'll need free space on your hard disk for your MP3 music files.

How much free space will you need? Well that depends on three things: how many songs you have (or plan to have), how long those songs are, and what bit rate and sample rate you use to encode those songs. I have a 60 GB hard disk in my Mac, with about 50 GB of free space, so I'm in excellent shape. I can add several thousand additional songs before I even come close to filling it up.

Chapter 10 is all about bit rates and sample rates. It includes exercises so you can hear how bit rates and sample rates affect sound quality, and see how they affect file size.

If you have a gigabyte or two of free space, you're probably in good shape. But if you have less than that, you might want to think about a larger hard drive, an additional external hard drive, or some other form of disc- (or disk-) based storage (DVD-RW, CD-RW, or whatever).

If you have a CD-RW (or CD-R) drive, you can burn a CD full of MP3 files and then play the songs right from that CD-RW (or CD-R) disc. It's less convenient than having all your songs right there on your hard disk, but it does work.

Bit rate refers to the number of bits used by one second of audio. Bit rate is commonly expressed in kilobits per second (that's 1,000 bits per second), abbreviated as kbps.

When you encode a file from a CD (or an AIFF or WAV file) into a smaller MP3 file, iTunes lets you choose the bit rate (if you want to). The higher the bit rate, the better the sound quality; the lower the bit rate, the worse the sound quality. Bit rate also determines the size of the MP3 file. The higher the bit rate, the bigger the file; the lower the bit rate, the smaller the file.

Sample rate refers to how often samples are taken from the original music signal. Sample rate is expressed in kilohertz, abbreviated as kHz.

When you encode a file from a CD (or an AIFF or WAV file) into a smaller MP3 file, iTunes lets you choose the sample rate (if you want to). The higher the sample rate, the better the sound quality; the lower the sample rate, the worse the sound quality. Sample rate also affects the size of the MP3 file. The higher the sample rate, the bigger the file; the lower the sample rate, the smaller the file.

Optional Stuff

If you have everything listed above, you're now completely ready to start using iTunes. But if you want to take advantage of some of its neatest features, there are a few more things you'll need, such as a CD-R (or CD-RW) drive, blank discs to use in the drive, an Internet connection, and a portable MP3 player.

CD-R or CD-RW drive

You don't need a CD-R or CD-RW drive to use iTunes, but having one lets you create (burn) your own music CDs, which, in my humble opinion, is the best thing iTunes can do.

Most (or all) Macs these days have a built-in optical drive, whether CD-RW, combo, or SuperDrive. If yours is among them, you're golden—iTunes works flawlessly with all built-in Apple optical drives.

If you don't have a built-in CD-RW drive, don't panic. iTunes also works with a lot of third-party (not made by Apple) external CD-R and CD-RW drives that connect to your Mac using USB or FireWire.

Most high-performance CD-R and CD-RW drives connect with FireWire, though USB is fast enough for CD-R or CD-RW drives. FireWire drives cost more than USB drives, but burn discs two (or even three or four) times faster. Many drives have both USB and FireWire, which should be a consideration if you want to use the drive with more than one Mac (especially if one of the Macs doesn't have FireWire). I currently have an internal SuperDrive and an external FireWire drive, which you can see in **Figure 2.1.** My advice: Unless you're a speed demon or have money to burn, a less-expensive USB CD-R or CD-RW drive may be a more prudent choice.

This is what a FireWire port looks like (bottom). Above it is the FireWire logo.

FireWire is a technology invented by Apple that is used to connect high-speed external devices such as digital video camcorders, hard disks, printers, and scanners to your Mac. FireWire is used industry-wide, and is also known generically as IEEE 1394 (Sony calls it iLink).

Figure 2.1 This is my external CD-RW drive, made by QPS (also known as Que).

Just my luck—QPS recently filed for bankruptcy protection. Sigh.

Any Mac that supports iTunes has USB ports. But many Macs also have FireWire ports, used to connect high-speed devices. And a FireWire drive can burn discs faster than a USB drive.

Not all external CD-R and CD-RW drives are supported by iTunes. You'll find the current list of supported external drives at www.apple.com/itunes/compatibility on Apple's Web site.

Though Apple's Web store (store.apple.com) sells several of the supported drives, you can probably find the same drive at a lower price elsewhere. Try Outpost.com (www.outpost.com), MacWarehouse (www.macwarehouse.com), or MacConnection (www.macconnection.com) for starters.

If your drive doesn't appear on the list, it may still work with iTunes. Many users have reported that their drives work with iTunes, even though they aren't on the list. So if you already have a CD-R or CD-RW that's not on the list, go ahead and try burning a disc—it just might work.

But if you haven't purchased a CD-R or CD-RW drive yet, you should definitely get one that *is* supported. That way you can be sure it will work properly with iTunes.

Blank discs ("blank media")

If you have a CD-R or CD-RW drive, you'll need some blank CD-R discs if you want to burn music CDs. Almost every computer store (including Web and catalog stores) carries blank CD-R media, but there are a couple of things you should know before you buy.

> **C or K?**
>
> Is that a d-i-s-k or a d-i-s-c? What's the difference?
>
> Generally, CDs and DVDs are called discs with a *c*, and other types of disks—floppy disks, hard disks, Zip disks—are disks with a *k*. Who am I to go against the grain?

First, you can store up to 74 minutes of uncompressed audio on a single CD-R disc.

When you shop for blank discs, you may see some that hold 80 minutes of audio. While they may work, Apple warns, "For greatest compatibility you should only use 74-minute media." If 6 extra minutes of music matters that much to you, go ahead and try some 80-minute discs, but don't blame me if they don't work. Another thing to consider is that 80-minute CDs may not work in older audio CD players, but a 74-minute disc probably will.

If you insist on trying 80-minute discs, don't buy a stack— buy one or two first to establish whether they work. If they do, then you can try a larger quantity. I've had good luck with the black Memorex 80-minute/700 MB discs.

Second, stick with brand names you've heard of, such as Kodak, TDK, and Fuji. Stay away from non-branded or store-branded discs (don't risk Bubba's DISCount Discs, Circus City Super-SpecialDiscs, or whatever). While the cheaper discs may work, a lot of them will probably fail during burning, resulting in what CD-R aficionados affectionately call a "coaster."

That's "coaster," as in the thing you put under a drink to keep it from leaving a ring on the table. A CD-R that fails during burning can be used as a coaster, a dangerous little Frisbee, or art, but not a whole lot else.

If you're bound and determined to use the cheap discs, just buy a few at first and make sure they don't turn into coasters. If they work out, then, and only then, should you buy a spindle of 50 or 100.

Bulk packages of blank CD-Rs are known as "spindles." That's because 50 or 100 discs come stacked on a little pole called (surprise!) a "spindle." Discs on a spindle are less expensive than discs packed in individual plastic "jewel cases," but of course that means they don't come with little plastic cases. Fortunately, most stores that sell spindles of blank CD-Rs also sell empty jewel cases. Some stores also sell inexpensive CD-sized envelopes. If you buy discs by the spindle, give some thought to where you're going to store them after you burn them.

Cables (external CD-R and CD-RW drives only)

If you want to use an external CD-R or CD-RW drive, you'll need the appropriate USB or FireWire cable to connect it to your Mac. While most external drives include the proper cable, some do not. So if you're buying a drive, make sure it comes with a cable. If it doesn't, be sure to buy one. If you don't, you'll be sorely disappointed when you get home and can only use your new drive as a paperweight.

Internet connection

You don't *need* the Internet to use iTunes, but you probably want it.

When you insert a CD, iTunes can look up song titles automatically using CDDB. You can download millions of MP3 files with programs such as Napster and from a number of Web sites (all of which we'll talk about in Chapter 8). You can listen to streaming Internet audio and radio stations, and

CDDB is a service provided by Gracenote, a company based in Berkeley, California, that delivers over the Internet information about audio CDs, such as album names and song titles. I love this feature and I think you will, too. If you want to know more about the service, visit the Web site at www.cddb.com.

purchase spoken-word content from Audible.com. Finally, you can email songs to friends and vice versa.

But all this magic is only possible if you have an Internet connection.

Speakers

You don't need external computer speakers to use iTunes, but since most Macs have lousy speakers, your music will sound a lot better if you invest in a set of decent speakers and connect them to your Mac. We'll talk more about speakers in Chapter 12.

Portable MP3 player

A portable MP3 player is like a Sony DiscMan that plays MP3 files instead of CDs. You use a USB or FireWire connection to transfer MP3 files from iTunes to the player. Apple's iPod is the Rolls Royce of portable MP3 players.

Unlike CD-R and CD-RW drives, every portable MP3 player I've ever seen includes the proper USB cable (and a pair of headphones, too).

Most portable MP3 players are tiny (3 or 4 ounces) and use flash memory cards to hold 30 or more minutes of music. Prices start well under $100.

iPods measure the amount of music they can hold in days, not hours! Mine's holding 3.9 days' worth right now and there's plenty of space left for more! They cost more than common MP3 players, but you really get what you pay for.

But the cheapest MP3 players come with 8 MB flash memory cards that hold a dozen songs...if you're lucky. Caveat emptor.

With one of these babies, you can listen to your favorite music anywhere, anytime. We'll talk more about portable MP3 players in Chapter 12.

That's it for the warm-up—let's roll up our sleeves and get to know iTunes a little better....

The iTunes Guided Tour

Now that you have a bit of background, it's time to roll up your sleeves and dig in. Don't get too itchy just yet. We're going to start off nice and easy, with a quick overview of iTunes. Think of this chapter as a warm up, to get you acquainted with iTunes; then, in upcoming chapters, we'll actually *do* the very cool stuff.

You don't have to be in front of your Mac while you read this chapter, but you might want to be. A lot of things in this chapter beg to be tried, and you can't try things in iTunes if you're not in front of a Mac.

Most of the items in this chapter aren't covered in depth. Don't panic: Almost every feature (and menu, for that matter) will be covered in breathtaking detail as you progress through the next few chapters. In fact, by the time you finish Chapter 7 you'll know more about every centimeter of iTunes than most people outside of Cupertino, California (Apple's hometown).

Overview and Tour

First, fire up iTunes and get comfortable. When iTunes is running, its main window looks like **Figure 3.1,** more or less.

If you haven't installed iTunes yet, this would be a good time to read Appendix A. It details the installation process and explains what the iTunes Setup Assistant is all about.

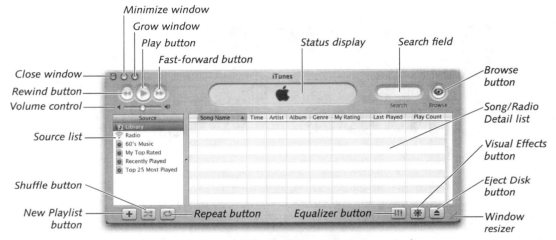

Figure 3.1 An annotated view of the main iTunes window.

I say "more or less" because if you've added songs to your Library, modified iTunes preferences, or created playlists, your window might look slightly different. (And yours probably doesn't have all those little lines and words.)

Now let's look at each of the items that make up the iTunes interface, so neatly pointed out in the figure above. There's no particular logical order here, so we'll just go clockwise from the top, starting with the Status display.

Status display

It doesn't look like much in the picture, but check out the Status display right there in the middle of things. Through this handy little porthole iTunes tells you what it's doing, and shows different information depending on the task at hand.

If you're playing a song, the Status display shows the name of the artist, the song title, and the album name. These three things "toggle" when you click them. In other words, if you click on whichever one is showing, it changes to another one. Click again and it changes again.

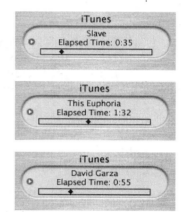

If a picture is worth a thousand words, these next few pictures are going to save you a lot of reading. Here's a closer look at the Status display showing a song title ("Slave").

Click directly on the song name, "Slave," and it instantly changes to the album name, *This Euphoria.*

Now click directly on the album name, *This Euphoria*, and it instantly changes to the artist's name, David Garza.

The second line of the Status display is also a toggle. Click it to toggle from Elapsed Time (how much of the song has played), which is what's shown in the three previous pictures, to Remaining Time (how much of the song is left), and then Total Time (the length of the song), as shown in the two pictures below.

The little diamond on the bar beneath the second line (the timeline, if you will), shows you how far "into" the song you are. If the diamond is all the way to the left, you're at the beginning of the song. If the diamond is in the middle of the bar, you're in the middle of the song. And so on.

If you click in this bar while a song is playing, you'll imme-diately jump to that point in the song. So if your favorite part of a song is the last 30 seconds, click three-fourths of the way over to the right and you'll jump right to that part. (Well, you'll jump somewhere near there, assuming the song is roughly 2 minutes long.) And you can drag the diamond back and forth to find just the perfect spot. Or to create really annoying noises....

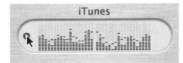

There's one other cool place to click in the Status display: the little triangle in a circle on the far left side. Clicking on this triangle makes a little graphic equalizer appear. I suppose it's displaying audio levels for the various frequencies in the song that's playing, but since there are no labels to tell you what each column represents, it isn't a very useful tool. Still, it's kind of fun to watch the columns "dance" in time to the music. Give it a try.

If you're listening to an iTunes radio station, the Status display shows the name of the station and how long you've been tuned in. (Clicking on the name of the radio station or on the elapsed time bar doesn't do a darned thing.)

Finally, if you're importing a song from an audio CD, the Status display shows the name of the song, the time remaining until it's done, and how fast the import is proceeding.

In the picture above, the import speed is expressed as "4.5x"—that means 4.5 minutes of song was being imported per minute.

Search field

The larger the music collection (of MP3 files) on your hard disk, the more useful this little field becomes. The Search field is easily the fastest way to find a song in your Library.

The "Library" is simply iTunes's term for the collection of MP3 files on your hard disk. More specifically, it refers to the files in your iTunes Music folder, which is in the OS X–created Music folder (in your Home folder) by default. You'll learn how to change the location of your iTunes Music folder (if you so desire) in Chapter 7.

Just type a word or words into the Search field and the Detail list instantly shows only songs that have that word or words in their title or artist's name, as shown in **Figure 3.2.**

Figure 3.2 When I type "dave" in the Search field, the Detail list below shows every song in my Library that has the word "dave" in its title or artist's name.

It's simple and it's lightning fast. The bigger your collection of MP3 files grows, the more you're going to love (and need) the Search field. When you want to see all of your songs again, just delete everything you typed in here.

Browse button

The Browse button gives you the option of "browsing" through your Library or playlists by category. When you click it, the main window changes, adding columns at the top of the window that let you filter your library or playlist by various categories.

As you can see in **Figure 3.3**, mine is set up to show Genre, Artist, and Album. (Compare **Figure 3.3** with **Figure 3.1**, which has no browsing columns.)

Click any item in one or more of the Browser columns. In a moment, only songs that match that item (or items, if you click more than one) are displayed in the song list.

In **Figure 3.3** I've selected "Austin" in the Genre column and "All" in the Artist and Album columns. So this song list is showing every song in my collection in the Austin genre.

The Genre column isn't available by default. If you want a Genre column in your iTunes browser, you'll need to enable it in the iTunes Preferences dialog box (which you'll learn about in Chapter 7).

In the following two chapters you'll learn more about your song list, your Library, and how to edit the description of a tune.

Figure 3.3 The iTunes main window after you click the Browse button.

Song/Radio Detail list

The Detail list displays information about whatever item is selected in the Source list (the leftmost column). So if you select Library as the Source, the Detail list shows all the songs in your Library (unless you're using the Browser columns or Search field to filter the list). If you select Radio, the Detail list shows Internet radio stations. If you select a playlist, the Detail list shows all the songs in that playlist (unless you're using the Browser columns to filter the list).

You can choose which columns you want to see in whichever list is being displayed here by choosing View Options in the Edit menu or by Control-clicking the name of any column to see the pop-up contextual menu.

As you can see by comparing **Figure 3.3** with **Figure 3.4,** the columns with a checkmark will appear in the Detail list; the columns without a checkmark won't.

Figure 3.4 These are your column choices for the Detail list as seen in the View Options dialog box (top) and the contextual menu (right).

To select a song in the Detail list, click on it so it's high-lighted. To select several songs, hold down the Command key and click them one after another. To select several songs in a row, click the first one, hold down the Shift key, then click the last one. All the songs between the first and last song you click will be selected. Put another way, you use the Shift key to make a contiguous selection, and the Command key to make non-contiguous selections.

Window resizer

You've seen them before, but the window resizer in iTunes looks a bit different. The window resizer is the little doohickey you use to enlarge or shrink the main iTunes window. Click on it and hold the mouse button down; now drag it around until the window is the size and shape you want.

The resizer works on a minimized iTunes window, too. If you drag it all the way to the left, you end up with a teeny, tiny window that shows only the command buttons.

Eject Disk button

If there's an audio CD, CD-ROM, or DVD in your internal or external optical disk drive, clicking this button ejects it.

You can also eject a disc by choosing Eject CD from the Controls menu or using the keyboard shortcut Command-E.

Visual Effects button

This button is pure, unadulterated fun. Click it and iTunes generates colorful random moving images in the place of the Detail list, as shown in **Figure 3.5**.

OK, so they're not very colorful in this picture. But that's not my fault—there's no color anywhere in this book except on the cover! Try it, though, and you'll see just how colorful the Visual Effects can be.

If you enjoy this kind of thing (I do! I do!), Visual Effects has scads of options you can play with. The most useful ones are available by clicking the Options button.

Figure 3.5 The iTunes Visual Effects are pure fun!

The Options button is in the upper-right corner of the window, where the Browse button was until you clicked the Visual Effects button.

The Visual Effects options are "Display frame rate," "Cap frame rate at 30 fps," "Always display song info," "Use OpenGL," and "Faster but rougher display." The frame rate tells you how fast Visual Effects are being blasted onto your screen, expressed in frames per second (abbreviated as fps).

Turning on "Display frame rate" will display the current fps in the upper-left corner of the Visual Effects display as seen in **Figure 3.5.** Visual Effects slow down some computers. If you find that happening to you, check the "Cap frame rate at 30 fps" check box to limit the number of frames per second to 30 or fewer. Song info means the MTV-like text showing the current song, artist, and album ("Long Way Down," Michael

Penn, and *Free For All* in **Figure 3.5**) in the lower-left corner of the display. "Use OpenGL" renders the display using OS X's built-in 3D display technology, OpenGL. Selecting this option should make the effects run smoother, but only if your Mac's video card supports OpenGL. Some older G3 models don't. Finally, since Visual Effects can slow down some computers, you can turn on the "Faster but rougher" display option. This will make the display look (can you guess?) a little rougher, but it will run a little faster. If the Visual Effects you're seeing seem sluggish, try it.

Song information always appears for a few seconds when you first turn on Visual Effects or when a new song begins, regardless of whether the option is enabled.

But that's not all you can tinker with! Visual Effects has other options that you can adjust "on the fly" (without opening the Options dialog box), by pressing certain keys on your keyboard. Just press the question mark key on your keyboard and a list of them will magically appear in the effects display.

If you press the question mark a second time, while the list is showing, you'll see additional options.

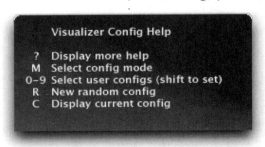

The iTunes Visuals menu has even more options. You can use it to turn Visual Effects on and off, you can select the size of your effects (as long as it's small, medium, or large), and you can choose to display your Visual Effects full-screen. This menu also displays a pair of useful keyboard shortcuts: Command-T toggles Visual Effects on and off, and Command-F displays them full-screen. The full-screen display is quite impressive if you aren't using your Mac for anything else at the time. (To get rid of the full-screen Visual Effects, either click the mouse button anywhere or press the Esc key on your keyboard. But be forewarned: The next time you turn on Visual Effects they'll still be in full-screen mode unless you choose a different mode from the Visuals menu first.)

> *The full-screen mode, while nice to look at, changes your monitor's resolution to 640 x 480, which may rearrange any icons on your desktop and reshape or resize any other windows you have open.*

I'll talk about Visual Effects in greater detail in Chapter 7.

Equalizer button

Click the Equalizer button to show the graphic-equalizer window, as seen in **Figure 3.6.**

Figure 3.6 The Equalizer lets you fine-tune frequency response.

Click the red Close button to put it away.

> *I'll talk more about this wonderful tool in Chapter 7.*

Repeat button

This button provides two different repeat functions. If you click it once, so it's highlighted, it plays every song in the current list once, and then starts over.

If you click the button a second time, it repeats the current song over and over.

When Repeat is turned off, the button looks like this.

Shuffle button

Click the Shuffle button to play the songs on the current list in random order.

Use the left and right arrow keys on your keyboard to skip to the next or previous song. I love this feature. If a song I don't feel like hearing comes on, I press the right arrow key and a new one is selected at random. Or, if I just have to hear that song one more time, I press the left arrow key and it starts again. Neat! Another nice touch that's new in version 3 is a preference that lets you choose whether to shuffle by song or by album. Whee!

New Playlist button

Click this button if you want to create a new playlist. There's much to be said about playlists. But since Chapter 5 is all about them (and the Library), that's all I'm going to say for now.

Source list

The Source list allows you to choose from among your Library, Radio, and any playlists you've created. To choose an item in this list, click it once.

To choose an item in the Source list and open it in its own window, double-click instead of single-clicking.

We'll go into more detail about the various sources in later chapters. You'll just have to be patient.

Volume control

You've surely used something like this before. It controls the volume for iTunes. Click the little "knob" and drag it to the left to make the volume softer; drag it to the right to make the volume louder.

Back button

Like the similar-looking button on a CD player (or a cassette player, for those of you old enough to remember them), this button takes you "backward" in the current song, if a song is playing. Press and hold the button to rewind. If you single-click on the Back button (rather than clicking and holding it), it jumps to the start of the current song. Single-click it again and it jumps to the start of the previous song.

If no song is currently playing, but a song is selected (high-lighted in the Detail list), clicking this button will take you to the previous song in the list.

If you've enabled Shuffle, the previous song will be another song in the list, but not necessarily the one directly above the currently selected song.

If no song is selected in the Detail list, the Back button is "grayed out," and can't be used.

Play button

Click this button to play whatever's currently selected in the Detail list. If no song is selected, but there are songs displayed in the Detail list, clicking the Play button will play the first song in the list.

If you've enabled Shuffle, a song will play at random, which means it probably won't be the first song on the list.

Forward button

As with the Back button, this button does what its lookalike on a CD player (or a cassette player, if you can remember those) does. It takes you "forward" in the current song, if a song is playing. Press and hold to fast-forward. If you single-click the Forward button (rather than clicking and holding it), it jumps to the start of the next song.

If no song is currently playing, but a song is selected in the Detail list, clicking the Forward button takes you to the next song in the list.

If you've enabled Shuffle, the next song will be another song in the list, but not necessarily the one below the currently selected song.

If no song is selected in the Detail list, the Forward button is "grayed out," and can't be used.

Close button

Clicking the red Close button closes the main iTunes window but doesn't quit iTunes.

There are many other ways to close the main window, too. You can choose Close Window from the File menu or choose iTunes from the Window menu. Or you can use the keyboard shortcuts Command-W for Close Window or Command-1 for iTunes window. Do any of those when the window is closed, and it will reappear.

Zoom button

Click the green Zoom button and the iTunes main window shrinks to a more manageable size.

Click and hold the mouse button anywhere in the shrunken window except the Status display to drag it anywhere on your screen. (Clicking in the Status display will still change what you see there.) When the window is where you want it, release the mouse button.

If you're using a Mac OS 9 version of iTunes (version 1 or 2), the Zoom button is a Zoom box, and is at the top-right corner of the window.

Minimize button

The yellow Minimize button works just like it does in every other OS X program. It stashes iTunes in the Dock until you need it again. The program is still running, but it displays no windows onscreen until you click its icon in the Dock to bring it back to life.

*The iTunes pop-up menu in the Dock, shown in **Figure 3.7**, is different from the usual menus in the Dock. When iTunes is running, its Dock menu lets you play, pause, or repeat the current song and skip forward or back in the playlist, right from the Dock. It also tells you which song is playing and allows you to rate it, right from the Dock. Nice touch, eh?*

Figure 3.7 iTunes' special Dock menu even works when the iTunes window is hidden or stashed in the Dock.

If you're running OS X, how do you know which version of iTunes you're using? If you launch iTunes, the OS X version won't cause the operating system to go into Classic mode. Another clue is if you see the classic rainbow-colored Apple icon in the upper-left corner of your screen while running iTunes in Mac OS X—that means you're using the OS 9 version. Finally, the OS X version has those "gumdrop" buttons; the OS 9 version has little boxes.

If you're running Mac OS X and you don't have version 3 of iTunes yet, hustle over to the Apple Web site and download it at once. It works a lot better with OS X than the Classic version and has some very cool features not found in the older OS X native versions.

Good Help Is Hard to Find

iTunes doesn't have a manual. And though that may be good news for me (maybe I'll sell more books), it isn't such good news for you. Fortunately, though Apple forwent the manual, iTunes does have a reasonably good Help system. Better still, if you've ever used Mac OS Help, you're already familiar with how iTunes Help works. But don't worry, I won't just leave it at that. Here's a quick lesson in how the iTunes Help system works.

Using iTunes Help

First choose iTunes Help from the Help menu, or use the keyboard shortcut Command-/ or Command-Shift-/ (either will work). This calls up the iTunes Help window.

*Check out the Keyboard Shortcuts menu item shown in Figure **3.8** when you have a minute. It's worth it.*

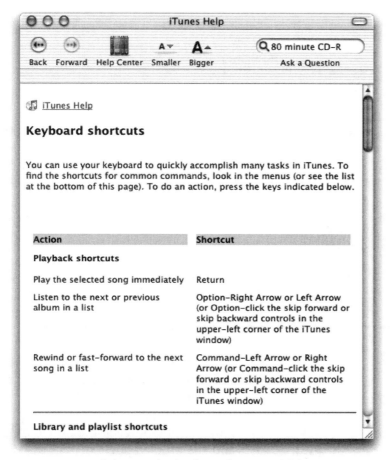

Figure 3.8 And that's only the first of six screenfuls!

Type a word or phrase into the text field, then click the Ask button. I was interested in whether or not you can use 80-minute CDs with iTunes. So I typed "80 minute CD-R" into the field then clicked Ask. In a few seconds, iTunes Help showed me a list of the articles that might answer my question.

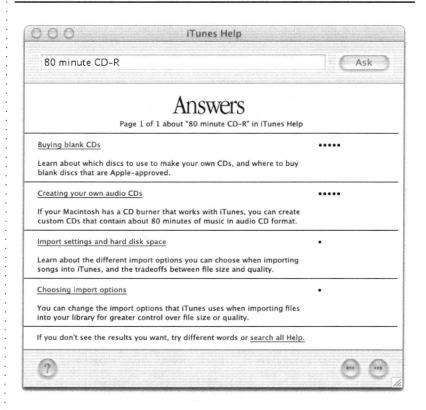

In this case, it found four articles. As you can see, the first article in the list is called "Buying blank CDs." It has five dots and it sounds like what I'm looking for. So I click the article title, and the article appears.

And guess what? That's exactly what I wanted to know. According to iTunes Help, 80-minute CD-R discs can indeed be used with iTunes.

If you're wondering, the left and right arrow buttons at the top of the window take you to the next or previous Help page you viewed, just like in a Web browser.

If you're using OS 10.2, your results page may look a little different, but it works pretty much the same way. The bar in the Relevance column tells you how relevant that article is to your search. The shorter the bar, the less likely the article is relevant, though it may be worth looking at anyway.

The OS 10.2 Help Center is more integrated than the older Help versions, and has a couple of interesting new features. The little icon that looks like library books opens the slide-out drawer showing all the Help topics available in your Help Center. It's also highly customizable—choose Customize Toolbar from the View menu in the Help Center. For example, I added the Smaller and Bigger buttons, which increase and decrease the font size in articles (but unfortunately not in lists). All of this wonderfulness can be seen in **Figure 3.9**.

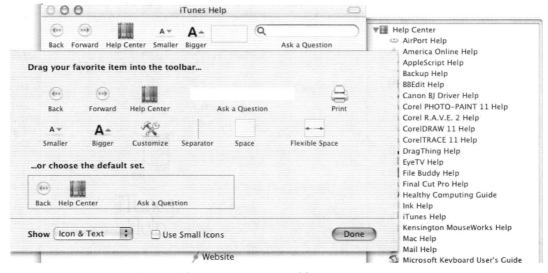

Figure 3.9 Even your iTunes Help view is customizable in OS 10.2.

Tool tips

In addition to the searchable iTunes Help, there are also pop-up "tool tips." When you point at certain things and hold the cursor perfectly still for a second or two, a little floating tip window pops up and tells you what you're pointing at.

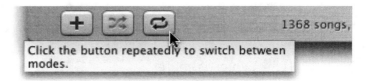

Alas, there are only a handful of them in iTunes—maybe a dozen things have tips attached. And as you can see in the picture above, the descriptions are terse.

Let's be honest here: Tool tips only work for about half the stuff in this chapter, and my descriptions are better. But I had to let you know they're there if you want them.

Unlike the Rolling Stones or Aerosmith, who just don't know when to stop touring, I do. This tour is now officially over (though I hear there's a big demand for a few more paragraphs in Japan!). So get ready to get your hands dirty.

part two

Working with iTunes

Ripping Songs

So why would you want to rip songs (also known as "import-ing" songs) from a CD? As I've said several times, MP3 files are roughly one-tenth the size of songs on an audio CD (or of songs you've ripped from an audio CD into AIFF or WAV files). So ripping songs from a CD into MP3 files lets you store ten times as many of 'em on your hard disk, which, as you'll see, is a very good thing.

If storing lots more music isn't enough for you, there's another good reason to convert CDs to MP3s: convenience. Once your songs are ripped and the MP3 files are on your hard disk, you can do a lot with them. Here are just a few of the things you can do.

- **Listen to any song with one or two clicks of the mouse.** When the song is on a CD, it's a hassle. You have to find the CD, eject the CD-ROM that's in your Mac, wait for the audio CD to mount, launch iTunes or Apple CD Audio Player, choose the track you want to hear, and so on. With MP3 files and iTunes, you just select the song and then either double-click it or click the Play button, and it starts up immediately.

- **Find any song in seconds.** With the Search and Browse features of iTunes you can find any song in your collection in a number of ways: by title, artist, genre, or just by good old-fashioned poking around.

- **Create playlists and Smart Playlists.** Playlists let you choose the songs you want to hear, then play them in sequence or randomly with no further intervention on your part. (You'll learn more about both kinds of playlists in Chapter 5.)

- **Use them in your iMovies and iDVDs.** If you can rip it, it can be in your movie or DVD without further ado. Drag and drop and you're done. Sweet, isn't it?

- **Create custom CDs.** Finally, iTunes lets you create custom audio CDs from the MP3 files on your hard disk. Most store-bought CDs have tracks you don't care for, but with iTunes you can burn CDs that have only songs you like, or burn CDs with a single song from a dozen or more different artists. And, in my humble opinion, this is the best feature of all. (You'll learn about burning CDs in Chapter 6.)

That's the *why*, now let's get to the *how*.

Unlike previous chapters, the rest of this chapter has tutorial instructions that you'll want to try yourself. I strongly recommend you read it sitting in front of your Mac, with iTunes running.

Getting Ready to Rip

First you need something to rip. So insert your favorite audio CD in your CD-ROM drive and wait a few seconds for it to mount on the desktop. (You do have iTunes running, right?) At this point, one of the following two things will happen.

1. The CD will appear as a generic "Audio CD," as shown in **Figure 4.1.**

2. The CD will appear with its name and other information displayed, as shown in **Figure 4.2.**

Figure 4.1 A "generic" audio CD with no information.

Figure 4.2 An audio CD with information.

A brief Internet interlude

If your CD looks like **Figure 4.1,** but you'd prefer it to look like **Figure 4.2,** don't worry. Most likely it's because the "Connect to Internet when needed" preference is turned off.

I'll show you how to change that in a moment, but first, let me say one thing: If you have a dial-up Internet connection, you probably don't want to enable this feature. If you do, your Mac will dial up your ISP and try to connect to the Internet every time you insert a new audio CD. Trust me—that's annoying.

On the other hand, if you have an Internet connection that's "always on," such as DSL or a cable modem, you definitely want to enable this feature. It's a great convenience.

iTunes has the ability to query a huge database of information about audio CDs (known as "CDDB") over the Internet, and automatically look up information for the audio CD in your drive.

I'll tell you a bit more about CDDB in Chapter 8.

To tell iTunes whether or not to connect to the Internet automatically whenever it needs to, choose Preferences from the Edit menu or use the keyboard shortcut Command-Y. Now click the General icon at the top of the window and check or uncheck the little box next to "Connect to Internet when needed," as shown in **Figure 4.3.**

Figure 4.3 This is how to tell iTunes to connect to the Internet and look up information about CDs automatically. Or not.

The rest of the Preferences dialog box is covered in detail in Chapter 7.

But even with this feature disabled, you're not out of luck. You can still ask iTunes to look up information about a CD at any time. First, enable your connection to the Internet (dial up your ISP, if you have to). Now select the CD in the Source list, and choose Get CD Track Names from the Advanced menu. In a moment, the track names, artist, album name, and, for most CDs, the genre will appear in the Detail list.

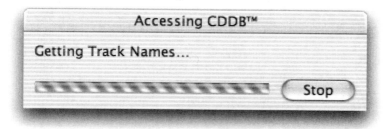

The CD icon on your desktop will also display title and track names, but not the artist, song lengths, or genre.

That just about does it for preparing to rip. Now, let's rip!

The Actual Act of Ripping

First, make sure the CD you want to import is selected in the Source list—it should be highlighted and the Detail list should display its contents.

 If you have an Internet connection and haven't yet gotten the CD track names, as described above, you should do that before you import the songs. Otherwise you'll have to type these things in yourself. Yuck. (For what it's worth, iTunes will provide the song length even if you don't Get CD Track Names.)

Now you're ready to rip, as long as you want to rip the entire CD. But if you only want to rip some of the songs, there's one additional step: choosing the songs you want to import.

When you insert an audio CD, iTunes automatically puts a checkmark next to every song. Each song with a checkmark will be imported (see **Figure 4.4**). To turn the checkmarks on or off, click directly on the check box.

Figure 4.4 Songs that have checkmarks will be imported; songs that don't have checkmarks—8, 11, and 14 (because I don't care for dust or blondes)—won't.

You only need to mess with the checkmarks if you don't want to import the entire CD.

Let it rip!

OK, it's that time. And wait 'til you see just how easy it is.

To rip all the songs with checkmarks, click the Import button at the top-right corner of the iTunes window.

If your button doesn't say "Import," click the name of the CD in the Source list to select it. (If the Library is selected in the Source list, it's the Browse button; if the Radio is selected, it's the Refresh button; and if a playlist is selected, it's the Burn CD button.)

Now sit back and relax for a few minutes.

If you want to watch the process (it's kind of like watching grass grow), there are a few things to look at.

- The Status display reports the time remaining until the current song is done importing and the speed of the import (in this case, 8 seconds and 10.3x, respectively).

Don't be alarmed if you're not getting 10x performance. I have a dual 1 GHz Power Mac with 1.5 GB RAM, so my setup rips as fast or faster than almost all others.

- A song that has been successfully imported gets a little green circle with a checkmark next to its name.

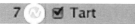

- The song currently being imported is marked by a little yellow circle with a wavy line next to its name.

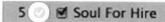

I know the icons look quite similar in the pictures above. They're really not—they look different on a color monitor. Even if the wavy line and the checkmark do look alike, you know that yellow means "currently being imported" and green means "imported successfully." And the yellow wavy line is animated (which lets you know something is still happening with this song), but the checkmark is not (which lets you know this song is done).

When iTunes finishes importing a song (green, with a checkmark), it automatically adds the song to your Library.

And that's all there is to it. You now know how to import songs!

Beyond Basic Ripping

That really is all there is to it. You can now rip any song on any CD and add it to your Library. But I'd be remiss if I didn't at least mention a few other things before we move on.

Most of what I'm about to mention is covered in detail in other chapters, but I want to at least introduce them here, so you know they haven't been forgotten (and you can skip to those chapters now, if you are so inclined).

Where the MP3 files are

Imported songs are automatically added to your Library (which is covered at length in the next chapter). But where are the actual MP3 files stored on your hard disk? Good question! And the answer depends upon which version of iTunes and which version of Mac OS you're using.

Under OS 9, they're in the iTunes Music folder (*not* the same folder the iTunes application is in), which is in the iTunes folder, which is in the Documents folder at the root level of your hard disk. (The "root level" of your hard disk is the level you see when you double-click the hard disk icon; it's also sometimes called the "top level.")

If you use Mac OS X and version 3 of iTunes, your MP3s are in the Music folder at the root level of your Home folder, not at the root level of your hard disk. (Actually, they're in the iTunes Music folder in the iTunes folder in the Music folder, but you get the idea.)

If you prefer to store your MP3 files elsewhere on your hard disk, it's no problem. You'll learn how to change their location in the "Preferences" section of Chapter 7.

It's best to keep all your MP3 files in the same folder (the iTunes Music folder, unless you change it). Otherwise, iTunes may have difficulty finding them in the future.

Encoding to file formats other than MP3

I mentioned before that *encode* means "convert a file from one format to another." So far all I've covered is encoding CD audio files into MP3 files. While this is what iTunes does by default, you can also encode a WAV file into an AIFF or MP3 file, an AIFF file into a WAV or MP3 file, or a WAV file into an MP3 or AIFF file just as easily.

Rather than explain it twice, I'll refer you to the "Preferences" section of Chapter 7 for the details of how to do all that.

Quality vs. file size

Another thing I should mention is that iTunes lets you adjust the quality (and thus, the size) of the files you rip. In this chapter we relied on the default settings, which nicely balance sound quality and file size, and should be just right for most people most of the time.

But iTunes *can* encode files that sound better (which makes them bigger) and files that are smaller (which makes them sound worse). It's a thorny issue and no two users agree on what settings are "best." I'll explain how it all works, as well as how to determine which settings are best for your needs, all in Chapter 10.

Editing song information

You've ripped some songs and they're in your Library, but you're not happy with the artist, title, genre, album title, or other information that iTunes grabbed from the Internet. Or you don't have Internet access, so they're still titled "Track 1," "Track 2," and so on. No problemo. You can change all of that.

Chapter 5 shows you everything you need to know about editing song information in your Library and playlists (and much more). So, without further ado, let's get to it!

All About the Library and Playlists

As I mentioned in Chapter 3, the Library is iTunes's representation of all the MP3 song files on your hard disk (or at least all the MP3 files it knows of). To iTunes, there is only one Library.

A playlist is any collection of songs you select from the Library. You can have as many playlists as you like, and each playlist can contain as many songs as you like. (Although, as you'll see in the next chapter, when you want to burn a playlist to CD, you'll want to limit the length.)

The Library and playlists are similar in many ways, but there are a few notable exceptions. So first we'll look at the features of the Library, then we'll make some playlists including some of the nifty new Smart Playlists. Finally, we'll delve into some tips and tricks that work in all of 'em.

No Card Required!

As you saw in Chapter 4, when you rip songs from a CD, iTunes automatically puts them in a folder called iTunes Music and adds them to the Library. And iTunes 3, by default, copies every file you add to the Library to the iTunes Music folder automatically (though you can turn this feature off in the Advanced pane of the Preferences dialog box).

The iTunes Music folder—which, if you haven't moved it, should be in the Music folder in your Home directory (OS X) or the root-level Documents folder (OS 9)—is an excellent place to store *all* your MP3 files, even ones you didn't rip from a CD yourself. Though you don't *have* to store all your MP3 files in a single folder, you probably should. If you store them in a bunch of different folders strewn around your whole hard disk, iTunes may not be able to find them again.

If you'd rather store your MP3 files in a folder other than iTunes Music, that's OK, just as long as you let iTunes know where it is. There's a Preference (also in the Advanced pane) you'll learn about in Chapter 7 that lets you designate any folder on your hard disk as your Library folder.

But even the most organized libraries sometimes lose things. If you try to play a song and get a dialog box like the one in **Figure 5.1,** click Yes and you can locate the file using the standard Macintosh Open File dialog box. But that's a hassle you'll avoid if you store all your MP3 files in the iTunes Music folder so they never become lost.

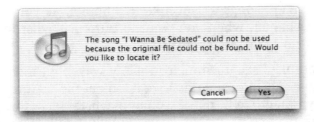

The song "I Wanna Be Sedated" could not be used because the original file could not be found. Would you like to locate it?

Cancel   Yes

Figure 5.1
The lost song dialog box.

Almost never. Every so often iTunes loses track of a song even though it is stored in the iTunes Music folder. If this happens to you, click the Yes button and find the song. Once you do it that shouldn't happen again.

In Chapter 7 you'll also learn about the Consolidate Library command, which can help you get all those MP3 files into the iTunes Music folder regardless of where they're stored now. But read the warning first—this action is not undoable.

Adding and deleting songs

There are two different ways to add a song or a folder full of songs to your Library. The obvious one is to use the File menu's Add to Library command; the less obvious (but often handier) one is to drag and drop your songs.

The obvious way

When you choose Add to Library from the File menu (or use the keyboard shortcut Command-O), a standard Open File dialog box appears, much like the one in **Figure 5.2.**

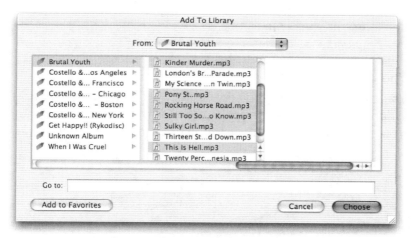

Figure 5.2 You can add a song or a folder full of songs to your Library with the Add to Library command.

In this dialog box, you can select a single song file, a folder full of songs, or a folder full of folders full of songs. When you click the Choose button, iTunes adds every selected MP3 file to the Library. So if you've selected a folder or folders, all the MP3 files in those folders will be added. Click Cancel to do nothing.

To select individual files or folders in this type of dialog box, press the Command key and click each file you wish to add. If the files or folders are contiguous (next to each other), you can click the first file or folder, then hold down the Shift key, and click on the last file or folder and the first, the last, and all the ones in between, will be selected.

The sidebar, "Selecting multiple items," coming up in a page or two, illustrates this concept. While the sidebar refers to items in the Detail list, the Command and Shift key work exactly the same way in iTunes Open File dialog boxes.

And that's it. The songs have been added to your Library.

The first few times you do it, you might want to open the iTunes Music folder and confirm that the songs are where they should be. They always are. If you added files from another disk or folder, you can delete them if you like because you know that you have copies of them, safe and sound in your iTunes Music folder. (And yes, the pun was intended.)

The other way

You can also add songs to your Library (or to a playlist) by dragging them in. Simply select the Library in the Source list and drag your songs onto the Detail list, as shown in **Figure 5.3.**

Figure 5.3 Dragging an MP3 file (or a whole folder full) onto the Detail list will add it to your Library.

You can also drag files or folders onto the Library or any non-smart playlist in the Source list as shown in **Figure 5.4.**

Figure 5.4 Dragging an MP3 file (or a whole folder full) onto the Library or a (non-smart) playlist, will add it to both the playlist and the Library.

To delete a song from your Library, select it in the Detail list and then press the Backspace or Delete key on your keyboard.

Polite program that it is, iTunes warns you before it deletes the file from the Library, as shown in **Figure 5.5.**

Figure 5.5 You can still change your mind about removing this file from the Library.

Click Yes to remove the item from the Library; click Cancel if you don't want to remove it.

Click the "Do not ask me again" check box before you click OK if you never want to see this warning again. (I predict you will click it soon.)

If the MP3 file is in your iTunes Music folder (as it should be, at least in my humble opinion), you'll see the additional dialog box shown in **Figure 5.6.**

Figure 5.6 It's already out of the Library, this box lets you get rid of it altogether.

Selecting Multiple Items

Both the Shift and Command keys are used to select multiple items from a list. But they don't work exactly the same way. It's helpful to understand the difference.

First the Shift key: If you click once, then hold down the Shift key, your selection will extend to wherever you click next. Selections made with the Shift key are contiguous, as you can see in **Figure 5.7.**

Now the Command key: If you hold down the Command key while you click an item, that item is added to the selection, which allows noncontiguous selections, as you can see in **Figure 5.8.**

Figure 5.7 Use the Shift key to select a block of items.

Figure 5.8 Use the Command key to select items anywhere in the list.

If you only want to remove the file from the Library's Detail list, and you want to leave it in your iTunes Music folder, click No. To move the file to the Trash, click Yes.

> *Don't be fooled by the Cancel button—clicking it is the same as clicking No. The song will still be removed from the Detail list (you already clicked Yes in the previous warning), but the MP3 file won't be moved to the Trash.*

> *One other thing: Undo won't undo moving a file to the Trash. If you want to undo that, you have to go to the Finder, open the Trash, and drag the file back to the iTunes Music folder. The file won't actually be deleted from your hard drive until you empty the Trash.*

> *The technique is the same if you want to remove several files at once from the Library. The only difference is that you have to select more than one item at the outset.*

Editing song information

Sometimes you add a song to the Library and discover it contains either no information or inaccurate information, like in **Figure 5.9.**

Figure 5.9 A song without information.

> *If you're not using CDDB to look up information about the songs you rip from CDs, all of your songs lack information!*

No worries. You can easily change that.

Select the song in the Detail list and choose Get Info from the File menu (or use the keyboard shortcut Command-I).

You can edit a song's info in the Library or in a playlist. It's the same either way.

A dialog box appears. Click the Tags tab and type in the missing info as I've done in **Figure 5.10.**

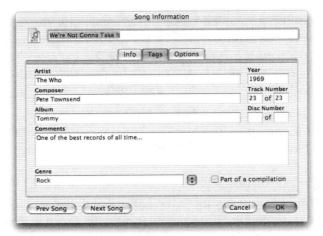

Figure 5.10 This is where you (manually) change the song information.

Click OK when you're finished adding and changing information.

If you want to edit the next or previous song, click the Prev Song or Next Song button instead of OK.

As you can see in **Figure 5.11,** the song in the Detail list now displays the information you typed so carefully into the Song Information dialog box.

Figure 5.11 The same song, but now with information.

While this type of editing changes the name of the song in your Library forever, the file on your hard disk will (unfortunately) remain named "Track 1" forever, too.

If you use CDDB when you import songs from CDs, this won't be a problem for you—the files will automatically receive meaningful and correct (usually) names.

Read this before you edit multiple songs

If you select multiple items in the Detail list and then choose Get Info from the File menu (or use the keyboard shortcut Command-I), you'll see a warning before the Song Information dialog box appears. The ever-polite iTunes will ask, "Are you sure you want to edit information for multiple items?"

Pay attention to this warning. And even though it offers a "Do not ask me again" check box, you might want to leave this particular warning enabled.

Editing multiple songs can have disastrous results if you're not careful. Let's say you select a dozen songs by different artists and then type just one character in the Artist field. You'll now have a dozen songs in your Library with that one character for their artist.

The song files on your hard disk still contain the proper original songs, only their information in iTunes—known as their "tags"—is messed up.

So be careful when you edit multiple songs. Though it's handy for giving songs the same genre, artist, or album, it's easy to goof up. I speak from experience.

Editing outside the box

There's another way to edit information for a song without using the Song Information dialog box, but it only allows you to edit one item at a time.

In **Figure 5.10,** I typed "The Who" as the artist. While that is correct, I later noticed that my other song by The Who doesn't have a "The," it's just "Who."

Because so many bands in my collection have names that begin with "The," I decided to change "The Who" to just plain "Who." And I'll do it that other way, without using the Song Information dialog box, so you can see how it works.

Click the song once to select it. Click again directly on the item you want to edit, in this case, the artist.

| ☑ Summertime Blues | 3:28 | Who | | Rock |
| ☑ We're Not Gonna Take It | 7:03 | The Who | Tommy | Rock |

A little box appears around the item you clicked (the words "The Who") to indicate that it is now editable. Edit to your heart's content, then click outside the little box or press Return or Enter.

If you click outside that little box or press Return or Enter before you're done editing, the item stops being editable. You have to select the song and click the item again before you continue editing. So don't click anywhere else until you're done editing.

You can see the result: no more "The."

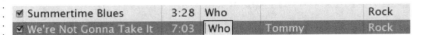

Here's another use for that little tidbit: when a column is too narrow to display the full title or artist's name.

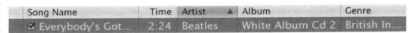

Click once on the song to select it, then click again on the specific item that's truncated by the narrow column. Our old friend the little box appears, bearing the full contents of that field.

Not only can you read the whole thing, but you can also edit any part of it. Not too shabby, huh?

Browsing the Library

The Library has one other unique feature—the Browse mode, which lets you filter by artist, genre, or album. It's easy, fast, and fun. We covered basic browsing in Chapter 3, but now we'll go into a little more detail.

The bigger your Library is, the more useful browsing is. If your songs are tagged with the correct information, it's a terrific way to sort through your collection. Conversely, if the song information is missing or incorrect, browsing will be essentially useless.

If you haven't added info for your songs yet (or had CDDB do it for you over the Internet), browsing is perhaps the best incentive to do so.

Browsing is easy: Just click the Browse button at the top right of the main iTunes window (or select Show Browser from the Edit menu or use the keyboard shortcut Command-B). When you Browse, the Detail list displays only songs that match the items selected in the Browser columns.

If you don't see a Browse button, make sure Library is selected in the Source list on the left. Browsing only works in the Library and playlists; it doesn't work with Radio.

My Library looks like **Figure 5.12** immediately after I click the Browse button.

Figure 5.12 The three columns of my Browser as they look immediately after I click the Browse button.

As you may remember from the tour in Chapter 3, when you first click the Browse button, "All" is selected at the top of all the Browser columns.

If you don't see a Genre column like mine, you can use the technique I showed you in Chapter 3 to get one.

At this point the Detail list displays every song in your Library. To actually browse your Library, you have to select at least one item in one of the Browser columns. The Detail list will instantly update itself to display only items that match your selection.

As you select items, the columns automatically update to reflect only those choices possible based on items you've selected already. So, for example, if I choose the Austin genre in the first column, only artists and albums that are tagged with the Austin genre appear in the second and third columns. And, of course, only songs tagged with the Austin genre appear in the Detail list, like in **Figure 5.13**.

Figure 5.13 When I choose the Austin genre, only Austin artists, albums, and songs are displayed.

When I click David Garza in the Artist column, you can see in **Figure 5.14** that the Album list (right column) displays only albums by David Garza, and the Detail list displays only the songs in my Library that are by David Garza.

David (pronounced "Dah-veed") Garza is one of my favorite Austin singer/songwriters. His first major-label release was This Euphoria. *If you like catchy, literate, hook-laden pop tunes played with rock-and-roll vengeance, you'll love it.*

And that's all you need to know about browsing. Have fun with it.

Figure 5.14 When I choose David Garza in the Artist column, only David Garza albums are shown in the Album column and only David Garza songs are shown in the Detail List.

Playing with Playlists

Playlists are mini-libraries you create yourself. While the Library contains all the songs iTunes is aware of, a playlist contains only the songs you specify. You can make as many playlists as you like.

Most of what you learned about the Library earlier in the chapter also applies to playlists. You select songs the same way. You edit song information the same way. The only major difference is that since the Browse button is now the Burn CD button, to browse a playlist you have to select Show Browser from the Edit menu (or use the keyboard shortcut Command-B).

Playlists group together songs in iTunes. The three basic reasons to do this are so you can listen to them (kind of like a CD but on your hard disk), so you can download the songs to a portable MP3 player, and so you can burn them onto an audio CD.

Now I'll show you how to create playlists and how to add and delete songs from them. We'll start with regular playlists before we move on to Smart Playlists, which are a whole 'nother story.

Creating and deleting playlists

You can create a new, empty playlist by clicking the New Playlist button or by choosing New Playlist from the File menu (or use the keyboard shortcut Command-N).

This is one of the sections where you'll probably want to have iTunes up and running so you can play along.

Or you can select songs in the Library and then choose New Playlist From Selection from the File menu (or use the keyboard shortcut Command-Shift-N). This creates a new playlist containing all the songs that were selected.

However you create it, your new playlist appears in the Source list and is named "untitled playlist." So the first thing you should probably do is give this playlist a name.

When it's first created, the name, "untitled playlist," is selected and ready to be edited. If you click anywhere else after creating the playlist (or if you need to rename a playlist you've already named), click the name of the playlist in the Source list once to select it, then click it again to make its name editable. Type a descriptive name for your playlist, then press Return or Enter.

To delete a playlist, click its name in the Source list to select it, then press Backspace or Delete.

Be careful: The Undo command (keyboard shortcut Command-Z) does not work for a deleted playlist. Once it's gone, it's gone. Poof!

Changing your playlists

There are two ways to add songs to existing playlists. You can drag them from the Library onto the playlist (as in **Figure 5.15** and **Figure 5.17**) or you can drag MP3 files from the Macintosh desktop onto the playlist (as in **Figure 5.16** and **Figure 5.18**).

And, interestingly, there are two ways to do each. Let's look at the less complicated way first: Drag a song onto the playlist's name in the Source list.

Figure 5.15 I'm dragging the song "S.R.V." from my Library to the Guitar Heroes playlist in my Source list.

Figure 5.16
I'm dragging the MP3 file of Meat Loaf's "Good Girls Go To Heaven (Bad Girls Go Everywhere Else)" from the desktop onto the 300 Pounders Plus playlist in the Source list.

You may have noticed that when you select a playlist in the Source list, its contents appear in the main iTunes window. If you double-click its name, the playlist will open in its own window. Then you can drag songs from the Library window onto the playlist window, as shown in **Figure 5.17**.

Last, but not least, you can drag an MP3 file onto a playlist window, as shown in **Figure 5.18**.

Figure 5.17 I'm dragging "Working Class Hero" from my Library onto the Songs w/bad words playlist's window.

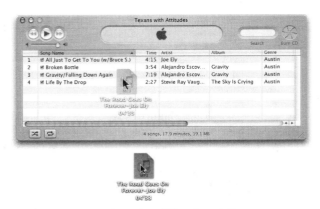

Figure 5.18 I'm dragging "The Road Goes on Forever" (by Joe Ely) MP3 file from the desktop onto the Texans with Attitudes playlist window.

*I used the desktop to illustrate my point in **Figure 5.16** and **Figure 5.18,** but you can drag an MP3 file from any location onto iTunes. It doesn't have to be on the desktop.*

So there you have it—an exhaustive list of ways to add songs to your playlists.

Now, what do you do if you want to remove a song from a playlist? Simple: Just select the song, then press Backspace or Delete. Poof. It's gone.

*When deleting a song from a playlist, you'll see the warning shown in **Figure 5.5.** This time it's no big deal—the song won't be removed from your Library, only from the playlist. If you later decide you want it back, just drag it into the playlist again.*

There's one last technique exclusive to the playlist that you need to know before we move on. That is, how to put songs in any order you like.

Make sure you have a playlist selected in the Source list or are working with a playlist in its own window when you try this next technique. It doesn't work with the Library.

First, click the column header above the song numbers, as shown in **Figure 5.19.**

If you click any other column header, such as Song or Artist, iTunes won't let you change the order of the songs.

Figure 5.19
Click here first.

If you've enabled the Shuffle button (it has a bluish glow), you can't change the order of songs either (which makes total sense when you think about it).

Next, select a song and drag it to a different position in the list, as I did with "Working Class Hero" in **Figure 5.20.**

Finally, release the mouse button when the song is at its new position. As you can see in **Figure 5.21,** "Working Class Hero" is now the last song in my playlist instead of the second.

Figure 5.20
Moving the song "Working Class Hero" to a new place on the playlist.

Figure 5.21
"Working Class Hero" is now the last song in the playlist.

You can move multiple songs the same way. Select them first—using either Shift, Command, or a combination of the two—then drag the whole bunch to wherever you want them.

And that's all there is to rearranging songs in a playlist.

Smarter Playlists

The second type of playlist is smarter—it can configure itself to your specifications, automatically selecting songs from your Library to populate itself. Pretty smart, eh? That's why they're called "Smart Playlists." Smart Playlists are so smart, they can even perform what they call "Live updating," which means they monitor your Library and modify their contents "on the fly" when you add or remove songs. Best of all, since Smart Playlists are nothing more than playlists with added intelligence, you already know pretty much how to use them (if you read the previous section, that is).

> *Smart Playlists are a wonderful, useful, smart feature; I recommend getting to know them if you have a large collection of songs in iTunes*

Smart Playlists are easy to create and even easier to use. Here are three ways to create a new Smart Playlist:

- Choose New Smart Playlist from the File menu.
- Use the keyboard shortcut Command-Option-N.
- Press Option and click the New Playlist button.

  When you hold down Option you'll see the New Playlist button's icon change from its usual state (a plus sign) to the special New Smart Playlist button icon, as shown in **Figure 5.22.**

Figure 5.22
The New Playlist button (top) becomes the New Smart Playlist button (bottom) when the Option key is held down.

All three techniques yield the same result—a window that looks like **Figure 5.23** opens.

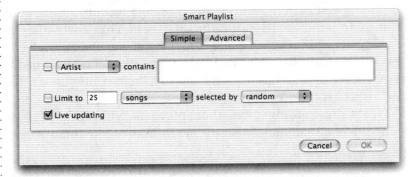

Figure 5.23 The Smart Playlist window as it appears when you first summon it.

Using Smart Playlists

The Simple tab of the Smart Playlist window offers simple choices:

- Include this: Artist, Composer, or Genre.
- Limit this playlist to [insert number here]: songs, GB (gigabytes), MB (megabytes), hours, or minutes.
- Select songs for this playlist: at random, by artist, by last played, by most played, or by song name.

Through the miracle of compositing in Photoshop, **Figure 5.24** shows all three of these pop-up menus.

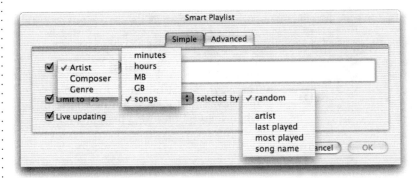

Figure 5.24 Three pop-up menus, two data-entry fields (name and number), and three check boxes are the entire Simple Smart Playlist lineup.

But if you really want to harness the power of Smart Playlists, you'll want to diddle with the Advanced tab, shown in **Figure 5.25.**

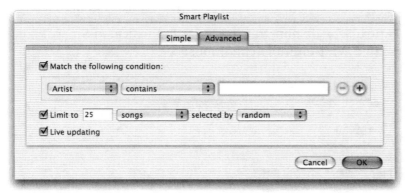

Figure 5.25 Notice the extra "contains" pop-up menu in the Advanced tab.

And once again, through the miracle of compositing in Photoshop, **Figure 5.26** shows the expanded pop-up menus for the Advanced tab.

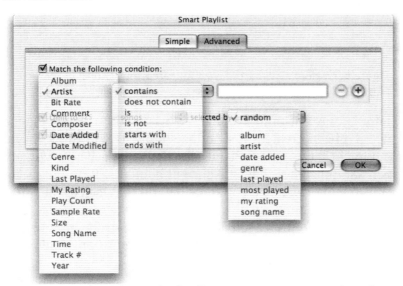

Figure 5.26 The Advanced tab offers many more options than the Simple tab.

 Most of the items are self-explanatory; if you need more info on how any of them work, choose iTunes Help from the Help menu and search for the item's name.

I saved the best part for last—when you use the Advanced tab, you can add as many criteria (or "conditions") as you like. To add a new condition, merely click the little plus symbol on the right; to remove a condition, click the minus symbol to its right.

Figure 5.27 demonstrates a more sophisticated Smart Playlist created with multiple conditions.

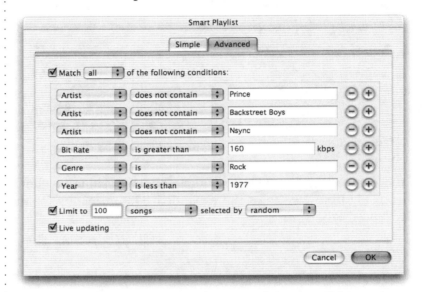

Figure 5.27 Here's a Smart Playlist I created that I consider particularly smart.

There is one last thing, though—how to edit a Smart Playlist once it's been created. It's not as simple as you think. If you double-click the Smart Playlist in the Source list, a window opens and displays the list's current contents. But what if you want to add or delete a condition? To do that, select the Smart Playlist you're interested in modifying in the Source list, then choose Get Info from the File menu (or use its keyboard shortcut, Command-I); the Smart Playlist configuration window for the selected item will pop open.

Smart Playlists and the iPod.

Smart Playlists work great on iPods, though live updates only occur when you connect the iPod to your Mac. Still, it's a great feature, and, in fact, if you're an iPod owner I'll bet you find yourself connecting just so your Smart Playlists will be updated. I know I connect mine far more often than I need to, just to get fresh tunes into my Smart Playlists.

Library and Playlist Tricks

Whew. We've covered a lot of ground in this chapter, but there are still a few more things you should know about working with lists. Now you'll learn some nifty techniques that apply to both the Library and playlists (Smart or not).

Views

iTunes is flexible about which columns of information are displayed in the Library or a playlist. To select which columns a list displays, choose View Options from the Edit menu (keyboard shortcut Command-J) while using that list. A dialog box like the one in **Figure 5.28** pops up with a bunch of check boxes that represent the columns available.

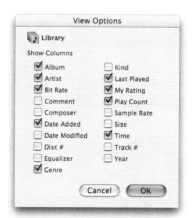

Figure 5.28
Checked items are columns that appear in my Library; unchecked ones aren't.

You can choose different View Options for the Library and for every playlist—just go through this process for each one.

The Song column is the only column that's mandatory. You can turn off all the other columns if you desire.

There's even a shortcut—Control-click the header of any column for a pop-up contextual menu, as shown in **Figure 5.29**.

Figure 5.29 Checked items will appear in my Library; unchecked ones won't—just like in the View Options dialog box.

The Auto Size Column and Auto Size All Column commands do what their names imply and are available only in this contextual menu.

Sorting lists

You can sort a list by any column. Just click once on a column header and the sorting is done. The highlighted column header displays a little triangle, as shown in **Figure 5.30**.

Figure 5.30 Select a column header to sort by that column; the little triangle tells you whether it's sorted backward or forward.

When the triangle points up, as it does on the left side in **Figure 5.30,** the list is sorted from A to Z or 0 to 9, based on the contents of that column. Click the column header once and the triangle flips to point downward; the list is resorted from Z to A (or 9 to 0) based on the contents of the column, as it does on the right side in **Figure 5.30.**

Working with columns

You can change the width of a column in the Library or a playlist by dragging the dividing line between any two columns. Move your cursor over the divider and it changes to a double-ended arrow as shown in **Figure 5.31.** Click and drag to enlarge or shrink the column.

Figure 5.31 I enlarged the Artist column by clicking the divider between Artist and Time (top) and dragging it to the right (bottom).

You can change the order of columns in the Library or a playlist, too. Click directly on a column header and drag to the left or right (while holding the mouse button). Drop the column (release the mouse button) wherever you want it, as shown in **Figure 5.32.**

Figure 5.32 Moving the Genre column from right (top) to left (bottom).

The Song column can't be moved. It's always the first
column in the Library or playlist, no matter what you do.

Searching

Last, but certainly not least, is the incredibly fast search function.
While browsing is great, when you want to find a particular song
in a huge Library like mine, the easiest and fastest way is to use
the Search field.

Just type a word or words into the Search field. You don't even
have to press Return or Enter. As you type, iTunes searches all the
columns for that word or words, and the Detail list displays only
songs that match.

To see all your songs again, delete whatever you typed in the
Search field.

You can even search and browse at the same time. For example,
if you've already filtered a list with the Browser (by selecting an
item from one of the Browser columns), and then you type something into the Search field, only the songs currently in the Detail
list will be searched.

OK, I think we've just about exhausted this subject. So let's
move along to the good stuff: In the next chapter I'll teach
you (gasp!) how to burn your own audio CDs.

Burning an Audio CD

6

If you haven't skipped any chapters so far, you now know everything you need to burn a CD. No, really: You really do know everything you need to know to burn an audio CD. You learned how to rip songs in Chapter 4, you learned how to create a playlist in the previous chapter, and you know where the Burn CD button is from the tour in Chapter 3. Click the button—that's all there is to it. You can move on to Chapter 7 now.

I'm kidding. It's *almost* that easy: You could just do all that right now and you'd probably end up with a usable CD. But there are a few details to attend to that will prevent frustration and ensure success. Remember, I said I could explain it to my dad in half an hour. Actually, it'll take less time. So I can assure you this chapter will be blessedly short and almost painless, even though it doesn't really end here.

This chapter really will show you everything you need to know to burn a great-sounding CD. But in Chapter 10 you'll get the rest of the story: compression, bit rates, sound quality, and file sizes. Though the iTunes default settings— as described in this chapter—will provide you with fine-sounding CDs, in Chapter 10 I'll show you how to actually test a bunch of different compression settings so you know for sure which sounds best to you. You should definitely read it before you burn too many discs.

The Preliminaries to a Successful Burn

Before you can burn a disc, you need three things: some songs in your iTunes Library, a supported CD-RW (or CD-R) drive, and a blank CD-R.

Songs

You can burn up to 74 minutes of music onto a standard blank CD-R, so you need to have enough songs in your Library to fill the CD before you attempt a burn. If you haven't ripped (or downloaded) that much music yet, you should do that before you proceed.

Unlike a cassette tape, once you record on a CD you can't go back and add more to it, so you'll want to have 60 or 70 minutes of music before you start burning.

CD-RW (or CD-R) drive

If your Mac has a built-in CD-RW drive, you're golden already and ready to rock. But if you have a third-party external drive, there are a couple of things to check before you begin.

First, make sure you have the latest version of iTunes. Version 1.0 didn't support third-party drives, so you'll need version 1.1 or later.

Version 3 supports even more third-party drives, which is yet another reason I recommend it over earlier releases.

The current version can be found at www.apple.com/itunes.

Make sure to get the right one for the system software on your Mac—there are different versions of iTunes for Mac OS 9 and Mac OS X.

If you aren't sure which system software you have, choose About This Computer or About This Mac from your Apple menu. And while you're checking stuff, you may want to check your iTunes version, too. To do so, choose About iTunes from the iTunes menu. Click the About window to make it disappear. It's usually a good idea to run the latest version (of both Mac OS and iTunes)—they're usually more stable and bug-free.

Second, make sure your external drive is supported by iTunes. Not all CD-RW (and CD-R) drives work with iTunes. If you're unsure about yours, check the list of supported drives at www.apple.com/itunes/compatibility.

Again, if your drive isn't on the list it may still work. But don't hold your breath.

Blank discs

I talked about blank media at some length in Chapter 2, so I won't repeat myself here. (Or at least not much.) The only thing I have to add is that since then I've taken my own advice and tried using 80-minute blank discs. All the 80-minute discs I've burned so far have worked perfectly. So even though Apple advises you to stick with 74-minute media, you may succeed with the 80-minute discs. I did.

Just remember not to buy 50 or 100 discs until you've tried a few and are sure they work with your particular setup. If they do work, when you go back for more make sure that you get the exact same kind you tested.

Burn, Baby, Burn!

OK. Let's go for it. I'll take you through the process step by step.

First, create a playlist that's a minute or two shorter than the disc you want to burn (no more than 72 minutes of music for the standard 74-minute discs and no more than 78 minutes if you're using an 80-minute disc).

Your playlist needs to be shorter because iTunes automatically inserts a 2-second gap between songs by default. I'll show you how to change this gap later in this chapter.

How do you know how long your playlist is? Just look for the total time at the bottom of the window, as shown in **Figure 6.1.**

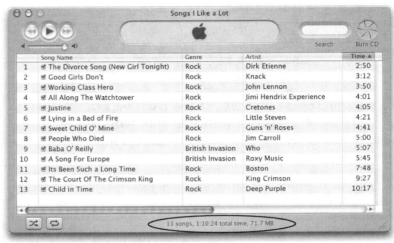

Figure 6.1 A playlist with 1 hour, 10 minutes, and 24 seconds of music (that's not quite 72 minutes), ready for burning.

The total time display at the bottom of *your* playlist window may not look like **Figure 6.1,** but may look like this instead:

13 songs, 1.1 hours 71.7 MB

Just click anywhere on the words as I'm doing above and they will automagically transform into the alternate display. Click again and they'll change back....

You can display the playlist in the main window or open a separate window for it—it doesn't matter.

If you put more music in your playlist than your disc can hold, iTunes will still burn the disc, but it will automatically stop after the last full song that fits. I usually allow one to two minutes per disc I burn for iTunes overhead, just to be safe.

Now click the Burn CD button.

The Burn CD button animates and takes on a different appearance, and the Status display tells you, "Please insert a blank CD."

Click the Burn CD button again. The Status display will explain what's going on as iTunes prepares the CD tracks.

iTunes automatically converts the MP3 files in your playlist into CD-DA files (which, as you remember, are the type of files used for audio CDs).

*Exactly how much time the preparation takes depends on the speed of your Mac's processor and the speed of your hard disk. On my G4 Dual 1 GHz it took less than a minute to prepare the songs in the playlist in **Figure 6.1** for burning.*

After a few other unimportant messages flash by, the Status display informs you that iTunes is now burning your CD.

You can cancel a burn at any time by clicking the little X next to the Progress Bar in the Status display. Be forewarned, though, that if you cancel after the preparation is complete and the actual burning has begun, you'll have to throw that disc away—it will be ruined.

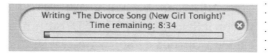

Exactly how much time the actual burning takes depends on the burn speed (sometimes called "write" or "writing" speed) of your CD-RW or CD-R drive. Mine burns at 8X, so it took just a little less than 10 minutes to burn this disc.

To get a rough estimate of your burn time, divide the total length of your playlist by the burn speed of your CD-RW or CD-R drive.

About 10 minutes after I clicked the Burn CD button for the second time, iTunes played a little musical riff to tell me my disc was done.

And that's all there is to it. Unless something goes wrong....

Troubleshooting Burns

The first thing I do after burning a disc is stick it into an audio CD player and listen to it from beginning to end.

Although you can use your Mac's built-in CD or CD-RW drive to check your new disc, if there's a problem, the drive could be part of what's causing it, so I think it's better to listen on a different CD player.

Every so often a song or songs will have some ickyness in it—skipping, static, popping noises, and such. If that happens, go back to your Mac and play the original MP3 file with iTunes. If the icky sound is in the MP3 file, rip the song again. If it's not in the MP3 file, try burning another CD. If the second CD has icky noises, try ripping the song from the original CD again, even if you didn't hear the ickyness when you played the MP3 file. If that doesn't fix it, there's almost certainly something more serious wrong with your software or your burner. Read on and try the following suggestions, even if they don't seem to apply....

"No burner or software was found"

If you clicked the Burn CD button and saw a message that said no burner or software was found, the problem could be one of three things.

1. Your CD-RW or CD-R drive isn't supported by iTunes.

2. The Apple CD-authoring software isn't properly installed or has been disabled.

3. Other CD-burning software (usually a program called "Toast," made by Adaptec/Roxio) is conflicting with iTunes. This particular issue is much less likely in OS X than OS 9, so using an OS X version of iTunes may be the easiest way to avoid the issue all together.

Toast 5.0.1 and later versions can get along with, and even enhance, Apple's CD-burning software. Earlier versions of Toast, alas, are likely to conflict with the Apple software. I'll tell you about Toast in Chapter 12.

If you have problem Number 1, you're pretty much out of luck—you need a supported CD-R or CD-RW drive. If you have problem Number 2, reinstall iTunes and restart your Mac. If you have problem Number 3, search iTunes Help for "burn," "no burner," and so on.

Burns that fail

If your burn fails in the middle, or if an inordinate number of discs seem to burn properly but then won't work in your audio CD player, there are a couple of things to consider.

First and foremost, make sure you are using good-quality, name-brand blank discs. (Remember what I said in Chapter 2 about cheap spindles of off-brand CD-R media?) Inferior media is the most likely reason for a burned disc not to work right. If you've only been using one brand of disc and are having problems burning successfully, try another brand.

If you've tried two brands of good-quality discs and still have problems, try burning at a lower speed. iTunes defaults to the maximum speed your drive can handle, but some drives can't really handle burning at their maximum speed. (What ever happened to truth in advertising?) To change the burn speed, choose Preferences from the Edit menu (or use the keyboard shortcut Command-Y), then click the Burning icon. Click the Preferred Speed pop-up menu and select a lower speed, as shown in **Figure 6.2.**

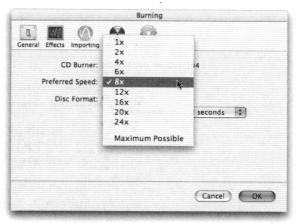

Figure 6.2 If you're having trouble burning discs, try a lower burn speed.

After you set iTunes to a lower speed, try burning a disc again. If you still have problems, try the lowest speed, 1x.

This panel of the Preferences dialog box is also where you change the gap between songs. As I mentioned earlier in the chapter, the default is 2 seconds, but you can make it shorter or longer with the Gap Between Songs pop-up menu, which is below the Preferred Speed menu, as shown in **Figure 6.3.**

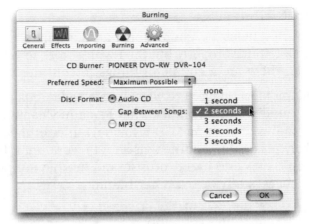

Figure 6.3 If you're jammed for space on the disc, try setting the gap between songs to none....

If you're still having problems, here are some other possible bugaboos—and what to do about them.

- Using other programs while burning could cause problems. Quit all applications except iTunes. Turn off file sharing and AppleTalk. Then burn again.

  Some programs in OS X run "in the background" and can't be seen or quit in the usual way. If all else fails, hold down the Shift key immediately after you log in to turn them all off temporarily. Then burn again.

- **A badly fragmented hard disk could cause problems.** Use a defragmenter like Norton Speed Disk or Alsoft PlusOptimizer. Then burn again.

- **A hard disk that's too old and slow could cause problems.** This won't be an issue for most of you—if you have a supported Mac (with USB), your hard disk is fast enough. But if you're using an older Mac, this could be your problem. Get a new Mac. Then burn again.

- **Your computer (or monitor) went to sleep while you were burning a CD.** To keep your system from going to sleep, increase the sleep timing settings in the Energy Saver pane of System Preferences. Search for "saving energy" in Mac Help for information about changing these settings.

Labeling Burned Discs

I intended to cover this topic in Chapter 12, but it occurred to me that you're better off hearing it now, before you delete the playlist for the disc you just burned. (Stick with me. You'll see what I mean in a second.)

So now you have a freshly burned disc, but there's no way to discern what's on it. Don't worry. There are a few things you can do about it.

You can buy a CD labeling system. I bought one called "CD Stomper Pro" that has four major components: software for creating label and jewel box artwork, label and jewel box templates, blank labels, and an applicator that centers the labels on your discs and presses them into place.

It sounds great, doesn't it? Too bad its Mac software is worthless—it crashes far too often and has an interface from H-E-double hockey sticks. Still, the kit was worth $25 for the Photoshop templates, the applicator, and the labels. When I'm feeling motivated I can make beautiful labels in Photoshop then apply them with the Stomper device. But most of the time that's too much work for me, so I've developed a quick and dirty technique for labeling my discs that I'll share with you now.

First, I write the disc's name (*Songs I Like A Lot* in the examples here) on the disc itself with a Sharpie fine-point marker, kind of like this.

Make sure you write on the back (dull) side of the disc. If you write on the shiny side (the side with the music), you'll mess the whole disc up and have to throw it away.

Then I take a screen shot of my playlist (Command-Shift-3) and open it in my graphics program (Photoshop). I crop out the extraneous portions and reduce it to 4.75 inches by 4.75 inches (the approximate size of a CD jewel box), so it looks like this.

The Divorce Song (New Girl Tonight)	Dirk Etienne
Good Girls Don't	Knack
Working Class Hero	John Lennon
All Along The Watchtower	Jimi Hendrix Experience
Justine	Cretones
Lying in a Bed of Fire	Little Steven
Sweet Child O' Mine	Guns 'n' Roses
People Who Died	Jim Carroll
Baba O' Reilly	Who
A Song For Europe	Roxy Music
Its Been Such a Long Time	Boston
The Court Of The Crimson King	King Crimson
Child in Time	Deep Purple

Finally, I print it, cut it out, and tape it into a jewel box. As long as I don't lose the jewel box, I know exactly what's on each disc. And I know which disc is which by the name I wrote on it with my Sharpie. It may be quick and dirty, but it's also fast, convenient, and cheap.

part three

Getting More out of iTunes

Inside iTunes

In previous chapters we've looked at iTunes with a view to getting things done, so menu items and preference settings were only described when they applied to the task at hand. This chapter is somewhat different—it's a comprehensive reference, not a how-to chapter. So if you want to know what a menu item does or how to configure a Preference setting, this is the chapter for you.

Since the title of this book includes the word *little,* and because I hate to repeat myself, I will refer you to other chapters if a topic has been (or will be) covered elsewhere. I'll only discuss a topic in this chapter if it isn't discussed at some length in another chapter.

First we'll look at every item in every menu, then we'll examine every item on every panel of the Preferences dialog box. And at the end of the chapter, I'll show you how to tweak the stunning iTunes Visual Effects (as I promised way back in Chapter 3).

We have a lot of ground to cover, so without further ado, allow me to present the iTunes menus.

iTunes Menus

iTunes packs a lot of punch into eight or nine relatively short menus. Let's look at them from left to right and top to bottom, starting with the iTunes menu.

The Mac OS 9 versions of iTunes have most of the same items in their menus as the OS X version, though they may be located in a different menu. This section describes the menu structure of iTunes version 3 for OS X.

Furthermore, the OS X version has an iTunes menu (actually the "application" menu in OS X parlance), which contains several Mac OS X–specific items that appear in every program's application menu. Those items—Services, Hide iTunes, Hide Others, Show All, and Quit—are not covered in this chapter at all.

Last but not least, if you don't have any AppleScripts in your Home/Library/iTunes/Scripts folder or you don't have a Scripts folder in Home/Library/iTunes, you won't have a Scripts menu in your menu bar.

The Application menu (a.k.a. the iTunes menu)

About iTunes displays a pretty picture with the version number, copyright information, and other stuff. Click anywhere on it to make it disappear.

It's mostly useful for when someone asks which version of iTunes you're using. If you don't know, this is where to look.

Preferences is the next menu item, but I'm going to skip over them for now and cover them in great detail in their very own section at the end of this chapter.

Why? Well, mostly because there are a lot of preferences and I think you'll be better able to "grok" them after you've become familiar with the contents of all the menus. Ergo, they appear last (but not least), in the section so imaginatively titled, "Preferences."

Shop for iTunes Products launches your Web browser and displays an Apple Store page hawking iTunes accessories.

Many of the accessories you'll see in Chapter 12 can be purchased here.

Caveat emptor. Apple sells everything at full list price. Many other vendors offer the same exact products at lower prices.

Provide iTunes Feedback launches your Web browser and displays an Apple iTunes Feedback form, as shown in **Figure 7.1**. If you have anything you'd like to say to Apple about iTunes, or if you've discovered a bug in the program, this is the best way to be assured someone at Apple is listening. (Probably.)

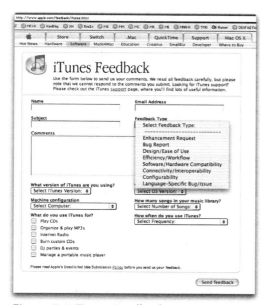

Figure 7.1 iTunes Feedback is new in version 3.0—and a welcome addition, at that.

The File menu

New Playlist (keyboard shortcut Command-N) creates a new, untitled playlist in the Source list (a playlist entitled, surprisingly enough, "untitled playlist").

The New Playlist button, described in Chapter 3 and shown here, does the same thing.

The tool tip shown above appears when you hold the cursor over the button for a few seconds. That's only half-a-tip, though; the other half is that for some items (including this one), if you hold down the Command key while the cursor hovers, you get an additional tip, like this:

New Playlist From Selection (keyboard shortcut Command-Shift-N) creates a new playlist from whatever songs are selected in the Detail list, as described in Chapter 5.

New Smart Playlist (keyboard shortcut Command-Option-N) opens the Smart Playlist dialog box (as discussed in Chapter 5). When you've made your selection and clicked OK, it creates a new, untitled playlist in the Source list.

iTunes, always trying to be helpful, may automatically name the new playlist for you based on the criteria you entered in the Smart Playlist dialog box (whether the Simple or Advanced tab). And iTunes is so polite, it automatically selects the text (in the Source list) of the name it chose for you, so you can change it immediately.

If you don't like the name, just start typing and your new name will replace it.

Add to Library (keyboard shortcut Command-O) brings up a standard Macintosh Open File dialog box, which you can use to select any MP3 file on any available disk or mounted remote volume, and add it to your Library.

Don't forget that if you haven't checked "Copy files to iTunes Music folder when adding to Library" in iTunes Preferences you won't be able to listen to this song unless that remote volume is mounted on your Mac.

Close Window (keyboard shortcut Command-W) does what all good Close Window commands do—closes the active (frontmost) window.

Import (keyboard shortcut Command-Shift-O) lets you import playlists you've exported previously using the next menu item...

Export Song List brings up a standard Macintosh Save File dialog box that lets you create a tab-delimited text file containing information about every song in the active list. That information includes name, artist, composer, album, genre, size, time, disc number, disc count, track number, track count, year, date modified, date added, bit rate, sample rate, volume adjustment, kind, equalizer, comments, play count, last played, your rating, and location. If you open it in a spreadsheet program such as Microsoft Excel or AppleWorks, it will look something like **Figure 7.2.**

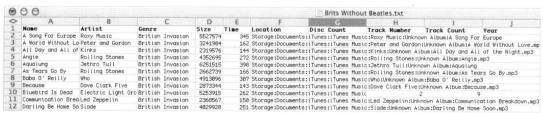

Figure 7.2 An exported playlist viewed in Microsoft Excel.

Export Library If you thought this command would do the same thing as the Export Song List command, you were wrong. Instead of spitting out an easy-to-deal-with tab-delimited text file, Export Library spews the contents of your iTunes Library as a gigantic XML (extensible markup language) document.

Get Info (keyboard shortcut Command-I) brings up the iTunes Song Information dialog box for the selected item or items, as described in Chapter 5.

Get Info is disabled (appears "grayed out" and can't be selected) when no items are selected in the Detail list.

What the Hell Is XML?

XML is a structured markup language (SML), used to organize and display documents containing a great deal of disparate information.

XML is very "in" these days—most of your Preference files (among other things) are stored in XML-formatted text documents.

Unfortunately, most applications haven't caught up with XML yet. I tried to open my Library.xml file in Microsoft Excel and it choked.

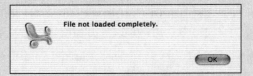

It seems that Excel can only handle 65,527 rows; my Library.xml file had more.

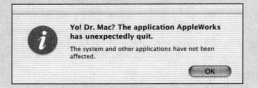

AppleWorks wasn't even that graceful. Unlike Excel, it couldn't even open part of the file; it just died unexpectedly:

TextEdit was able to open the file without a problem, but working with a text file of 60,000+ lines isn't fun.

So far the best thing I've found for viewing XML files is Apple's own Property List Editor application, available as part of the OS X Developer Tools installation.

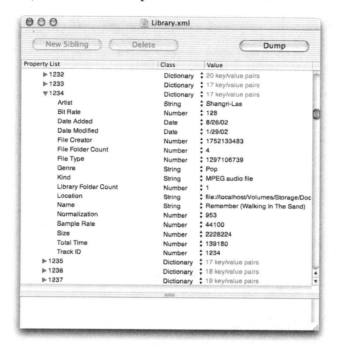

Show Song File (keyboard shortcut Command-R) locates the MP3 file (in the Finder) for the selected song in the Library or a playlist.

Memorize that keyboard shortcut: Command-R.

It's an excellent, useful command, and I'm pretty sure it isn't covered anywhere else.

This is a very good feature, and a real time-saver. Without it, I'd have to open five separate folders to get to "A Day In The Life.mp3" (which is on the Beatles' masterful *Sergeant Pepper* album).

Figure 7.3 I love this command—it's sweet.

Show Song File is also disabled if multiple items are selected in the Detail list (which makes complete sense, when you think about it).

Show Current Song (keyboard shortcut Command-L) finds the song iTunes is currently playing and selects it in the Detail list. Regardless of what window is currently active, iTunes goes straight to the Source for the current song—so if you're playing an Internet radio station while browsing your Library and you use Show Current Song, iTunes will change the selected Source from the Library to Radio.

This command is disabled when no music is playing (because there is no current song).

Burn Playlist to CD does just what you'd expect—it burns the selected playlist on a CD, just as though you had clicked the Burn CD button.

This command is disabled when no playlist is selected, and/or when the active window is not a playlist (for example, the Library or Radio).

Update Songs on iPod also does what you'd expect, but only if you have an iPod (it's grayed out if no iPod is connected). If an iPod is currently connected to your computer, choosing this command will update the iPod based on your selections in the iPod Preferences window, which appears when you click the little iPod button next to the equalizer button, like this:

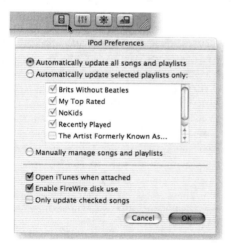

The button only appears when an iPod is connected. If none is connected, you'll see a blank space where you see the iPod button above.

The Edit menu

Undo, Cut, Copy, Paste, and **Clear** do the usual stuff, which, as they say, is "beyond the purview" of this book.

If you aren't sure what that stuff is, I have four words for you: The Little Mac Book. *It's by Robin Williams, it's excellent, and it'll help you master just this kind of stuff. (And no, my publisher didn't make me say that.* The Little Mac Book *truly is one of my favorites.)*

Select All (keyboard shortcut Command-A) selects every item in the active window. This command is disabled if the Source list is active (the Source list doesn't allow multiple selections).

Select None (keyboard shortcut Command-Shift-A) deselects every item in the active window. This command is also disabled if the Source list is active (the Source list doesn't allow multiple selections), or if no items are selected.

Hide/Show Browser (keyboard shortcut Command-B) toggles the Browser columns discussed so long ago, way back in Chapter 3. Select it to hide or show the Browser; select it again to do the opposite.

View Options opens a dialog box where you can choose which columns appear in a list. There are slightly different versions for the Library, for playlists, for Radio, and for audio CDs.

Which version you see depends on which list or window was active when you chose the View Options command.

Each playlist has its own View Options. So you can have different settings for every playlist (if you like).

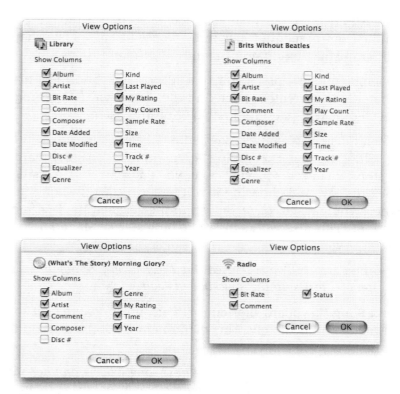

Figure 7.4 View Options for the Library (top left), a playlist (top right), an audio CD (bottom left), and Radio (bottom right).

The Controls menu

Most of the commands in this menu have either a button counterpart in the iTunes windows or a keyboard shortcut, or both. The Play button, Forward button, and Back button on every iTunes window (as shown and discussed in Chapter 3) do the same thing as the first three menu items in the Controls menu. The keyboard shortcuts I've listed (for all commands that have one) are even more convenient.

My point is that I rarely use the items in this menu. The buttons or shortcuts are more convenient.

Don't forget that fantastic and mostly complete set of excellent keyboard shortcuts. Choose Keyboard Shortcuts in iTunes' Help menu.

Pause/Play/Stop (keyboard shortcut spacebar) is the first item on the Control menu. It has three names because it's a shape-shifter, displaying different names at different times.

When no music is playing, it says "Play," and choosing it plays whatever is currently selected in the Detail list. (If nothing is selected, it will play the first song on the list.)

When music *is* playing, it says either "Pause" (for music files) or "Stop" (for Internet radio stations), and choosing it pauses or stops whatever is playing. After you pause or stop, it changes back to Play, and choosing it will either restart the song from where you paused, or reconnect to the selected Internet radio station. (This also works for audio books—like an audio book-mark, if you will.)

I don't think I've ever used this chameleon-like menu item—I just slap the spacebar instead.

Next Song (keyboard shortcut right arrow) starts the next song on the list immediately. This menu item is disabled when the Radio is active.

If you've enabled Shuffle, the next song will be another song on the list, but not necessarily the one below the currently selected song.

Previous Song (keyboard shortcut left arrow) immediately starts the previous song on the list or, if a song is playing, starts it over again. This menu item is disabled when you're listening to Radio.

If you've enabled Shuffle, the previous song will be the song you just heard, but not necessarily the one above the song that's playing.

Shuffle plays the songs in the current list in random order. When it's turned on you'll see a checkmark next to its name. This menu item is disabled when the Radio is active.

Repeat Off turns off the next two Repeat commands. When it's enabled you'll see a checkmark next to its name. Select-ing either Repeat All or Repeat One turns it off. This menu item is disabled when the Radio is active.

Repeat All plays every song in the current list once, and then starts the list over and plays them all again. When it's enabled you'll see a checkmark next to its name. Selecting either Repeat Off or Repeat One turns it off. This menu item is disabled when the Radio is active.

Repeat One repeats the current song over and over. When it's enabled you'll see a checkmark next to its name. Selecting either Repeat Off or Repeat All turns it off. This menu item is disabled when the Radio is active.

Volume Up (keyboard shortcut Command–up arrow) makes iTunes play louder.

Volume Down (keyboard shortcut Command–down arrow) makes iTunes play softer.

Mute (keyboard shortcut Command–Option–up or down arrow) makes iTunes silent. Choose it (or use the shortcut) again to un-mute.

Eject CD (keyboard shortcut Command-E) ejects mounted audio CDs.

The Visuals menu

I covered Visual Effects in Chapter 3. And I'll cover it again at the end of this chapter. Here's what the Visuals menu items do.

Turn Visual On/Off (keyboard shortcut Command-T) turns Visual Effects on or off. When they're off, this menu item reads "Turn Visual On." And vice versa. This menu item is disabled when any window except the main iTunes window is active.

Small displays Visual Effects in the main iTunes window at a small size.

Medium displays Visual Effects in the main iTunes window at a medium size.

Large displays Visual Effects in the main iTunes window at a large size.

Full Screen (keyboard shortcut Command-F) hides all iTunes windows (and all other windows) and displays Visual Effects on the entire screen.

This command is a toggle. When you turn it on it, a checkmark appears next to its name.

If you turn visuals on when there's a checkmark next to Full Screen, the visuals appear full screen (even if you see a checkmark next to Small, Medium, or Large).

Click the mouse button or press Escape to kill the full-screen Visual Effects and make iTunes (and all other windows) reappear.

Choose Full Screen a second time to turn it off and remove the checkmark.

There are some additional tips for configuring Visual Effects later in this chapter.

The Advanced menu

Open Stream (keyboard shortcut Command-U) brings up the Open Stream dialog box. Paste or type in the URL for an Internet radio stream then press OK.

Opening streams is covered in Chapter 9.

Convert Selection to MP3/AIFF/WAV converts the selected item to a CD audio, AIFF, WAV, or MP3 file. Select a song or songs in your Library or a playlist, choose this menu item, and a temporary playlist called "Converting Songs" appears; your songs will be ripped using your current Importing settings (see Chapter 10, and also the "Preferences" section later in this chapter, for more information).

Use the Command or Shift key to make multiple selections.

If no item is selected the Convert Selection to MP3/AIFF/WAV item is disabled.

Consolidate Library opens a little warning box that explains what's about to happen and reminds you that it can't be undone. If you have songs in your iTunes Library that are located anywhere but the iTunes Music folder, choosing this command will place a copy of all those song files in your iTunes Music folder.

Song files located outside the iTunes Music folder are not deleted—they are merely copied to your iTunes Music folder.

Be careful with this one. You could end up with a bunch of duplicates in your Library (and your iTunes Music folder), and this command cannot be undone.

Get CD Track Names looks up the track names, artist name, album name, and genre for audio CDs in CDDB, the giant audio-CD database. This menu item is disabled unless an audio CD is mounted.

This feature requires an active Internet connection.

Get CD Track Names and CDDB are covered at some length in Chapter 4.

Submit CD Track Names uploads track names, artist names, album names, and genres for audio CDs to CDDB. This menu item is disabled unless an audio CD is mounted.

This feature requires an active Internet connection.

After using Get CD Track Names you may discover mistakes, or you may want to add additional details to an entry. Make the changes in iTunes, then use this command to resubmit the information for the CD with your changes. Your version is compared to existing entries and the best parts of each are used.

Editing song information is covered in Chapter 5.

Join CD Tracks imports multiple songs from an album as a single track so you won't hear gaps between songs.

Add/Remove Audible Account lets you manage your account with Audible.com, a Web site that sells spoken-word content you can listen to in iTunes or on your iPod.

I'll tell you more about Audible.com in Chapter 8.

Convert ID3 Tags lets you change the ID3 format of tags. This menu item is disabled if no items are selected in the Detail list.

I've never had to use this feature. According to iTunes Help, "If a song's title and information don't appear correctly, the file was probably created using a program that stores information in a different way from iTunes. You may be able to resolve the problem by converting the song's information tags (ID3) to a different storage format."

The Window Menu

Minimize (keyboard shortcut Command-M) does what you'd expect—it stashes the active iTunes window in the Dock. Duh.

It's kind of sneaky—you can't get it to un-minimize by selecting the same menu item; to "maximize" a minimized window you have to click its icon in the Dock. Or you can select the iTunes menu item, covered below.

Zoom does exactly the same as clicking the green gumdrop button—either zooms the active window to full-size or shrinks it down to a little nub. Choose it again to do the reverse.

iTunes (keyboard shortcut Command-1) hides or shows the main iTunes window. Choose it again to do the reverse.

This menu item will also un-minimize iTunes if it's stashed in the Dock.

Equalizer (keyboard shortcut Command-2) hides or shows the iTunes graphic equalizer window. Choose it again to do the reverse.

Bring All to Front is a standard OS X command that brings all windows to the front when chosen.

In Mac OS X, activating a program doesn't always bring all of that program's windows to the front. In other words, you could be using iTunes but have one or more iTunes windows hidden behind other windows (Finder windows, other application windows, etc.). This command forces all open iTunes windows to appear in front of any other active application or Finder windows.

The Help menu

iTunes Help (keyboard shortcut Command-?) launches the iTunes Help program, as discussed in Chapter 3. Type in a word or phrase, then click the Ask button.

Click an answer ("Correcting song titles with odd characters," in the picture) to read more about that topic.

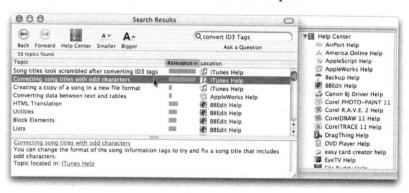

Preferences

In this section you'll discover the five panes of the Preferences dialog box. To follow along at home, open the Preferences dialog box by choosing Preferences from the iTunes menu.

Or avoid those pesky menus completely by using the handy keyboard shortcut Command-Y, which opens the Preferences dialog box.

General

Click the General icon at the top of the window to activate the General pane (if it isn't already active).

The **Source Text** pop-up menu lets you choose the size of text in the Source list; the **Song Text** pop-up menu lets you choose the size of text in the Detail list and playlists.

Your choices in both menus are Small or Large, as shown in **Figure 7.5**.

The **Show genre when browsing** check box adds a Genre column to your iTunes Browser.

See Chapter 5 for more about browsing your Library.

The **Connect to Internet when needed** check box determines whether iTunes connects to the Internet automatically when you insert a CD.

I'll just repeat what I said in Chapter 4. If you have a dial-up Internet connection, you probably don't want to enable this feature. If you do, your Mac will dial up your ISP and try to connect to the Internet every time you insert a new audio CD. On the other hand, if you have an Internet connection that's "always on," such as DSL or a cable modem, you definitely want to enable this feature. It's a great convenience.

Figure 7.5 Small (top) and large (bottom) text = size.

If you click the **Use iTunes for Internet Music Playback** button (it says "Set"), iTunes will launch automatically when you encounter an MP3 stream in your Web browser.

You may have configured this setting when you ran the Setup Assistant, as described in Appendix A.

The **On CD Insert** pop-up menu lets you choose what happens when you insert an audio CD. It has four choices, Show Songs, Begin Playing, Import Songs, and Import Songs and Eject. The choices are mutually exclusive: Pick one and that's what happens whenever you insert a CD.

Effects

Click the Effects icon at the top of the window to activate the Effects pane.

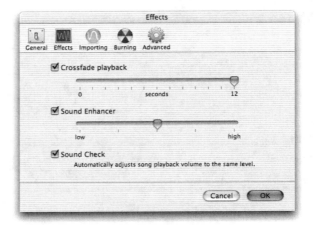

All three Effects in this pane are new in iTunes 3.

Crossfade playback makes one song fade smoothly into the next, without any silence between them. Crossfading is turned on by default.

Sometimes the ends of songs get cut off using the default crossfade duration of 6 seconds. If it happens to you and you hate it, choose a shorter duration or turn crossfade off altogether.

Sound Enhancer will (according to Apple), "add depth and enliven the quality of your music."

If you've ever had a stereo system with a Loudness button, you may know what to expect. Sound Enhancer performs a similar type of magic on your music, but is far more refined than those old "loudness contour" buttons that did nothing more than boost the highs and lows a bit.

The Sound Enhancer can be auditioned easily. Just pick a tune you like and open Preferences to the Effects pane. With the slider in the middle, click the check box, turning Sound Enhancer on and off. Hear that? Now, drag the slider right or left to increase or decrease the effect. Hear it?

I use it (set at about the halfway point, as shown in the picture), and I think it makes most songs sound much better on my particular setup.

Sound Check adjusts all the MP3, AIFF, and WAV files in your Library so they play at roughly the same volume level. In other words, you won't have to fiddle with the volume control for every song.

*If some songs in your Library are **VERY LOUD** and others are very soft, this command can be a blessing. On the other hand, if you have a lot of songs with delicate soft passages, you may find it offensive. I happen to like it and have used it happily since the day it arrived.*

By the way, it's even better on an iPod. Not only do you avoid fiddling with the volume control, but you never get your ears blown out by an unusually loud song.

Importing and Burning

Chapter 10 covers every aspect of the Importing and Burning preferences. There's nothing more to add here.

Advanced

The Advanced panel offers even more choices—where your iTunes Music folder will be located (on your hard disk), the size of your Internet radio buffer (cache), your preference in shuffling (by song or album), and two nifty options for keeping your iTunes folder organized.

In Chapter 3 I promised I'd show you how to change the location of your iTunes Music folder. Here's where I do it.

In the iTunes Music Folder Location section of the pane, click the Change button. A standard Macintosh Open File dialog box will appear. Navigate to the folder you want to designate as your iTunes Music folder, click the Choose button, and you're golden.

Well, you're golden unless you click the Preferences dialog box's Cancel button, which cancels your change.

The **Streaming Buffer Size** pop-up menu lets you choose the size of the buffer (or cache) for streamed Internet content. Your choices are Small, Medium, and Large. Medium is the default setting.

The buffer is a cache for the incoming Internet stream. Suppose you're listening to a radio station, but for some reason your connection is interrupted for a fraction of a second. If you were listening to the stream directly as it downloads, you'd hear a pop or even a blank space as the stream of music dried up. But with a buffer, iTunes has data in reserve (actually, it's cached on your hard disk), and can continue to play music while it frantically tries to reconnect to the radio station in the background.

If Internet radio stations stutter or hiccup, try a larger buffer.

Keep iTunes Music folder organized automatically creates sub-folders for artists and albums when you add songs to the library using the next feature.

Copy files to iTunes Music folder when adding to library automatically copies files to your iTunes Music folder whenever you add a song to the Library. So if you drag a song from the desktop to the Library window, iTunes will make a copy of that song and stash it in your iTunes Music folder. If you've also checked the box above this one, it will be stashed in the proper artist and album folder (if that information is available).

> *If the **Keep iTunes Music folder organized** check box is checked, and you edit a song's information after you import it, iTunes will automatically move the file to the proper folder or create the appropriate artist and album folders (inside the iTunes Music folder, of course), if necessary.*

> *The original song file (located outside the iTunes Music folder) is not deleted—it is merely copied to your iTunes Music folder automatically.*

One Last Look at Visual Effects

I waxed rhapsodic about Visual Effects for two whole pages during our tour in Chapter 3. But I promised you more, and more you will get! Here's a handy list of keyboard shortcuts and how to use them, followed by some useful information about plugging in new and different Visual Effects for free.

> *The default Visual Effects module (plug-in) is called the "iTunes Visualizer." You'll learn more about plug-ins after these Visualizer shortcuts.*

iTunes Visualizer shortcuts

These first two shortcuts work all the time, regardless of whether Visuals are on or off.

- **Command-T** toggles Visual Effects on and off.
- **Command-F** toggles full-screen mode on and off.

The following shortcuts only work when Visual Effects are on. Some of them appear in pictures in Chapter 3. This is how they work.

Unlike most keyboard shortcuts, these don't require the Command key.

- Pressing **?** or **/** displays a list of basic commands. Press it again for more help.

The next three shortcuts let you cycle through the Visualizer's preset display values. Three different presets make up each configuration.

I couldn't find official names for the three different presets. So I made them up. I think Behavior Modification, Color Modification, and Color Theme describe them well, though.

- **Q** and **W** cycle through the next and previous Behavior Modification presets, respectively.
- **A** and **S** cycle through the next and previous Color Modification presets, respectively.
- **Z** and **X** cycle through the next and previous Color Theme presets, respectively.

Each preset interprets music differently, so each one has its own unique look and feel.

When you press any of these keys, the names of the presets appear in the upper right corner:

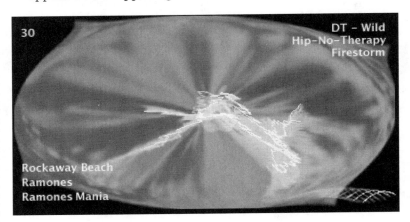

The top line is the Behavior Modification preset's name ("DT-Wild"); the second line is the Color Modification preset's name ("Hip-No-Therapy"), and the third line is the Color Theme preset's name ("Firestorm").

Press them all; press them often—these presets are one of the best parts of the Visualizer.

- **0** to **9** chooses a saved configuration. If you come across a particularly mind-boggling configuration, you can save it for future use. Press Shift together with one of the number keys (either the ones at the top of the keyboard or on the numeric keypad, as you prefer) to store the configuration under that number. Now any time you want to experience that same visual splendor again, press that number key with Visualizer running to bring it back.

Calling up a numbered configuration doesn't automatically display the configuration's name. You have to employ this next shortcut.

- **C** displays the current configuration's name.

- **R** shuffles the three presets to create a configuration at random.

This doesn't automatically display the configuration's name, either.

- **M** has the cryptic name "Select config mode." It chooses how iTunes switches from one configuration to another. Pressing the M key cycles through these three choices:

Random slideshow mode: iTunes chooses a random combination of presets, plays that configuration for a while, then switches to another configuration chosen at random.

User config slideshow mode: iTunes cycles through the configurations stored under the keys 0–9, displaying each one for a brief period of time.

Freezing current configuration: This knocks iTunes out of slideshow mode, so it stays with the current configuration until you instruct it otherwise.

- **F** toggles the on-screen frame-rate display (in the upper-left corner). Faster is smoother.

- **T** toggles frame-rate capping, in case it's too smooth. (Discussed in Chapter 3.)

- **I** toggles track information. (Also discussed in Chapter 3.)

- **D** resets all settings to their defaults.

Use this last one after using all the other commands and messing everything up. It will set all of your Visual Effects preferences back to their default values, so things will be as they were before you started mucking around.

So there you have it. I think you'll find Visual Effects even more enjoyable now that you know how to tinker with them.

Visual Effects plug-ins

But wait—there's still more. If you ever get tired of the built-in Visualizer, there are additional Visual Effects plug-ins that make the experience different and new again. And they're free!

You can find these little gems at your favorite Internet download site; search for "iTunes" and "Visual" or "plug-in." I found the ones in this chapter at www.versiontracker.com.

After you download and decompress a new plug-in, install it by following these instructions from iTunes Help:

- To install a plug-in for a specific user, drag the plug-in to the iTunes Plug-ins folder, located in the iTunes folder inside the Library folder in the user's home folder.

- To install a plug-in for all users of the computer, drag the plug-in to the iTunes Plug-ins folder, located in the iTunes folder inside the Library folder at the top level of your Mac OS X startup disk. You may need to create the iTunes and iTunes Plug-ins folders in this location if no previous system-wide plug-ins have been installed.

If the plug-in comes with a "Read Me" file, you really should read it. Some of them—like the about-to-be-mentioned ArKaos Visualizer—require you to put a bunch of stuff into the Visual Plug-Ins folder.

If iTunes is running, you'll have to quit and restart it before you can use your new plug-in.

Plug-ins appear at the bottom of the Visuals menu.

When you try out a new plug-in, don't forget to click the Options button and see what you find.

Sometimes the Options button brings up a dialog box with lots of neat options for you to play with.

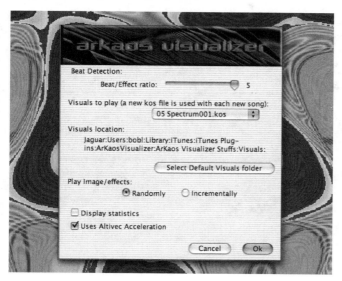

And sometimes it brings up a dialog box full of nothing.

Click the Options button anyway. You'll never know what you're missing (if anything) if you don't at least try it.

One other thing you might try is the Control-click. In the ArKaos Visualizer, for example, a contextual menu lets you choose one of the installed effects "on the fly," provides access to the Options window, and opens a connection to the ArKaos Web site, where you can get additional visuals to install.

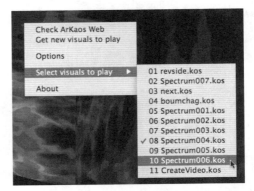

Last, but not least, here's what the ArKaos Visualizer plug-in looks like on screen:

And that, my friends, is what Visuals plug-ins are all about. I'm sure you'll enjoy many hours of entertainment with them.

I think you know iTunes inside and out by now, so it's time to move on. In Chapter 8, you'll learn how to find millions of different MP3 files on the Internet.

Music on the Internet

This is going to be a tough chapter to write. The state of downloadable audio content on the Internet (copyrighted commercial music in particular) is in flux as I type this. As you'll soon see, the Internet is currently a virtual smorgasbord of downloadable songs, most of which are provided by individuals and can be downloaded for free.

That almost certainly won't be the case much longer. The major record labels and the Recording Industry Association of America (RIAA) have put the original music-sharing service, Napster, out of business (more about that in a moment) and are still lobbying the United States Congress to enact legislation that will allow them to control what you download and where you can download it. The legal wrangling could go on for years and the final outcome is far from certain, but if the recording industry prevails, all forms of file-sharing service could be legislated out of existence.

Unfortunately, my editor says I have to turn in this chapter today, so what you're about to read describes the way things worked in the summer of 2002. Your mileage (and your costs) may vary.

Artists absolutely deserve to be paid for their work. But between you and me, I'd like to see the money go to the artists, not the record companies.

Sharing Files

One way to share files over the Internet is to exchange MP3 files as email attachments. But that requires at least one friend with MP3 files to share, and, unfortunately, not everyone has such a friend.

There is another way to share music—it's called "peer-to-peer file sharing" ("PTP" for short). The late Napster service was probably the best known, but many other similar services have sprung up, both before and since its demise.

In concept, PTP file sharing lets you make new friends and share music with them. With a peer-to-peer file-sharing service, you use special software to download files from other users' hard drives and to offer files on your hard drive to other users.

Though sharing your files isn't mandatory, it is considered polite if you're going to use the service.

In other words, there is no central server or Web site involved— you download the files directly from other users' hard drives. The service only provides the mechanism for sharing files; it doesn't offer any MP3 files itself.

Now that Napster is gone, the dominant service, at least for Mac users, is called "Gnutella." Gnutella is an open-source protocol, which means that there is no actual company behind the protocol. Taken a step further, that means the government and recording industry are having huge problems with it. It's not going to be possible to sue it the way they sued Napster— if nobody owns it, whom do you sue? So at least for now, nobody owns it, but it's out there in the ether, it works, and it's free.

To search for music on the Gnutella network you'll need a client program. The two best-known Mac clients are LimeWire (www.limewire.org) and Acquisition (www.xlife.org), shown in **Figures 8.1** and **8.2**. And, as befits an open-source protocol, both client programs are free.

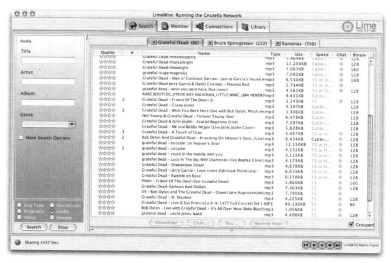

Figure 8.1 LimeWire has this ugly interface, but it works just fine.

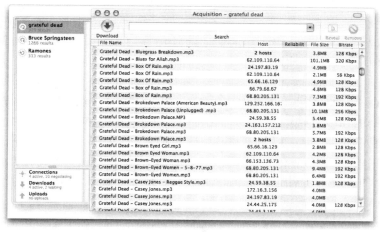

Figure 8.2 Acquisition's interface is more Mac-like, and it works just fine, too.

LimeWire also offers a Pro version, with improved through-put and no advertising, for less than $10.

After you download either program and install it, you'll be ready to search the Internet for MP3 files offered by other Gnutella users and download the files to your hard disk.

You need to have a "live" Internet connection to use a Gnutella client. So if you have a dial-up connection, be sure to connect before you try to use the software.

What's good about PTP

You search for a song by artist or title or both, and then download it to your hard disk. It's way cool—just think of a song you want to hear, and in a few minutes you can be listening to it. Let's see your FM radio do that!

What's bad and ugly about PTP

Peer-to-peer is not all sweetness and light. Since you're dealing with files created and offered by other users, there are some very real problems to contend with.

The quality of some songs is just plain lousy. I've downloaded songs with snaps, crackles, and pops in the middle of them, as well as songs that are incomplete.

Even if the quality is there, not every file is what it says it is. Just because a file appears to be the latest single from the Backstreet Boys, that doesn't mean it is. The only way to find out is to download the file and listen to it. I've downloaded files that purported to be songs I like, but instead contained 3 minutes of a demented dude laughing madly.

Because you're downloading from other users' hard disks, the service isn't always reliable. If that user disconnects from the Gnutella network or turns off their computer while you're in the middle of a download, you'll end up with half a song.

Finally, though you may argue that sharing songs with friends isn't illegal (which it may or may not be), it is almost certainly unfair to artists.

I hope the courts and record labels don't kill the whole sharing concept—it's just too cool. My wish is for them to figure out a way to charge for this incredibly convenient service and get that money into the hands of the artists. Even with the issues described above, I'd gladly pay a reasonable fee (per file or per month) for the ability to download songs I want to hear. It seems unlikely I'll get my wish, but that's how I'd have it work in a perfect world.

Music Web Sites

As you might expect, there are literally thousands of Web sites devoted to music, and many of them offer MP3 files for your downloading pleasure. In this section we'll take a look at a couple of the most popular, as well as others that are of interest to music fans.

Listen.com

Listen.com (www.listen.com, **Figure 8.3**) used to be (perhaps) the biggest site on the Web for music fans.

That should come as no surprise—it has raised more than $100 million in funding to date, some of it from the five big major record labels (BMG Entertainment, EMI Recorded Music, the Universal Music Group, Warner Music Group, and Sony Music Entertainment).

The site recently changed its name from Listen to Rhapsody though its URL remains the same. And while the new service refers to itself as the "Premier Digital Music Service," you'll have to downgrade your computer (to a Windows box) if you want to try it. As of this writing they offer no Macintosh support whatsoever, as shown in **Figure 8.3**.

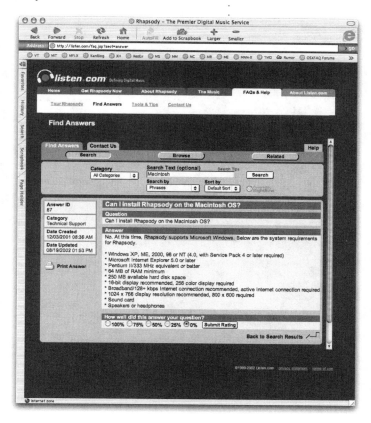

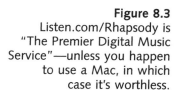

Figure 8.3
Listen.com/Rhapsody is "The Premier Digital Music Service"—unless you happen to use a Mac, in which case it's worthless.

There are other pay-to-download sites, including the highly touted PressPlay (www.pressplay.com), but few if any support the Macintosh. Yet.

It's no big deal yet, as none of the Windows-only sites offers more than a token selection of songs by a token selection of artists on a token selection of labels. You'll find no Beatles, no Stones, no Brittany, no Backside Boys, and so on. There is nothing even close to my dream site—a one-stop, pay-to-download site that offers most songs and artists in a single place— much less such a beast that's also Mac-friendly. This will change, of course, but for now we Mac users are pretty much left out.

I wouldn't lose sleep over it. I searched several of the Windows-only pay-to-download sites and found very few songs I like, and even fewer songs I'd pay to download.

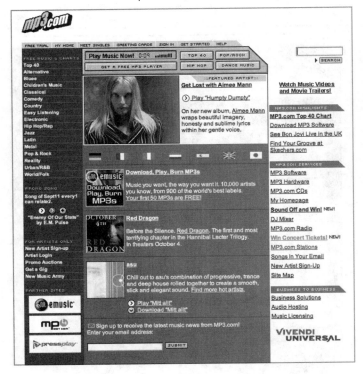

Figure 8.4 MP3.com: All MP3s, all the time.

MP3.com

Perhaps the granddaddy of MP3 music sites is MP3.com (www.mp3.com, **Figure 8.4**). MP3.com's archives (more than 900,000 free songs!) are searchable and categorized to make browsing easy.

Unlike some music-oriented sites you may encounter, MP3.com offers only MP3 files. Furthermore, MP3.com offers fewer popular songs and artists—instead, it specializes in unsigned and less-known acts. And since all the files are MP3s, it's Mac-friendly.

> *Sure you'll find some big names here—I saw free downloads by Madonna, Faith Hill, Aimee Mann, and other major artists. But most of the songs on MP3.com are by artists you've never heard of. That's not necessarily a bad thing—I've discovered plenty of great music by artists I'd never heard of before by browsing around on this site.*

MP3 search engines

There are dozens upon dozens of MP3 search engines on the Web, most of which claim to be "the most complete music search engine on the planet." The vast majority of them use "bots" and "Web crawlers" that automatically comb the Internet for files with the .mp3 suffix. These search sites have names like AudioPhilez (www.audiophilez.com) and "Mamma: The Mother of All Search Engines™" (www.mamma.com).

Just between us music lovers, I find most of these sites a waste of time. They're full of broken links, dead pages, inaccurate descriptions, and intrusive pop-up ads. If you don't mind that kind of thing, by all means give it a try—every so often you do strike gold. But frankly, I'd be surprised if any of them are still in business by the time you read this.

> *If this sort of thing appeals to you, try this: Go to your favorite "regular" search engine (www.ask.com, www.google.com, www.altavista.com, or whatever), and type in something like "MP3 search" or "music search engine." You'll find enough music and media search engines to keep you busy for a week. Of course, most of them will probably be a waste of time, but you won't know for sure unless you try. (If you find a great one, send me email—I'd love to hear about it!)*

Informative and entertaining music sites

If you're a music fan (and you probably are, since you bought this book), there other music-related sites worth knowing about. Given the pitiful state of downloadable music on the Web today, these are the sites that give me hope for the future of music on the Web. Here are some of my favorites.

Rolling Stone magazine (www.rollingstone.com, **Figure 8.5**) and the cable TV channels MTV (www.mtv.com, **Figure 8.6**) and VH1 (www.vh1.com, **Figure 8.7**) each have a comprehensive Web site that serves up more of what they offer in print and on TV. If you like the magazine or cable channel, you'll almost certainly love the Web sites.

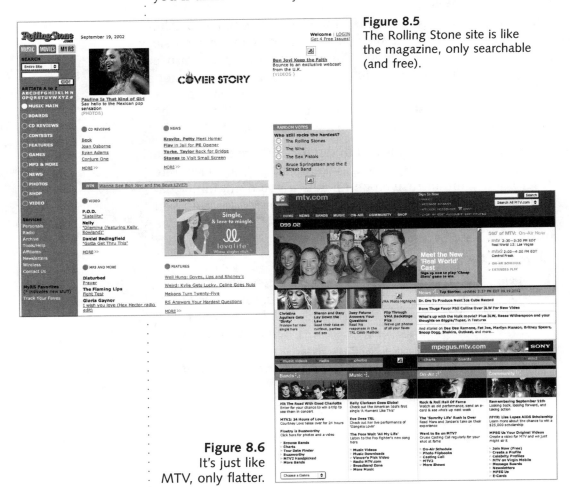

Figure 8.5
The Rolling Stone site is like the magazine, only searchable (and free).

Figure 8.6
It's just like MTV, only flatter.

Figure 8.7 VH1.com—a grown-up version of MTV.com.

Two other informative sites you might enjoy are Artist Direct(www.artistdirect.com, **Figure 8.8**) and the All Music Guide (www.allmusic.com, **Figure 8.9**). Both have huge searchable databases, chock-full of information about almost any musical artist you can think of.

Figure 8.8 Artist Direct is jam-packed with information on more than 100,000 artists.

Figure 8.9 The All Music Guide is just what its name implies.

Last, but not least, there's Gracenote (www.gracenote.com), which I introduced you to briefly in Chapter 2. As you may recall, this site maintains the CDDB, the database of track information iTunes provides when you insert a CD. In Chapter 4 I said that I'd tell you more about it later. Well, here it is.

CDDB is not a music seller nor does it offer MP3s, pictures, or videos. But it may be the largest music database on the Web, and you can search for all the songs and albums by an artist or find out what artists have recorded a particular song (as long as you know the song's name). If you can't find it here, chances are it's never been recorded.

Gracenote also offers links to news about artists, links to sites where you can buy their works new or used, plus links to artists' official Web sites (if they have one) and sites created by their fans (see **Figure 8.10**).

Figure 8.10 Gracenote's CDDB is great for finding other CDs by artists you enjoy.

While I find the database unwieldy at times, and often get hundreds of responses when I search for an artist or song, it also frequently points me to a song or artist I wouldn't have thought of otherwise. Which is why I say it's worth knowing about.

Audible.com

iTunes 3 includes a new books-on-electrons feature that lets you buy books on the Web at www.audible.com, download them to your Mac, and then listen to them with iTunes 3, on your iPod, and even burn them to an audio CD.

Being your faithful servant, I have thus far sampled three of Audible.com's books-on-MP3—*The Second Coming of Steve Jobs* (unabridged, 8 hours; $15.95) by Alan Deutschman; *21 Dog Years: Doing Time @ Amazon.com* (unabridged, 6 hours, 40 minutes; $17.95) by Mike Daisey; and *Robin Williams' Famous Friends* (2 hours, 51 minutes; $19.95).

The first two were read by their authors, which I liked. Who better than the author to read me a story?

The third was a collection of spontaneous and unscripted Robin Williams interviews with celebrities like Bonnie Hunt, Susan Sarandon, and Jeff Bridges not available in any other format—an Audible.com exclusive.

The service, shown in **Figure 8.11,** is easy to use and has received rave reviews in the press and around the Web.

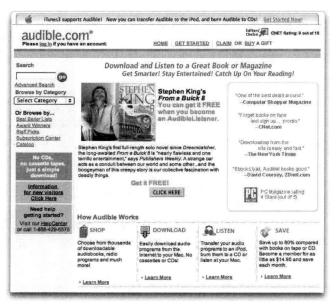

Figure 8.11 The Audible.com Web site is Mac friendly and easy to use.

When you buy a program from Audible.com, your purchases are stored in your own personal library on the Web for your convenience.

This is mine:

I downloaded all three to my Mac and loaded them on my iPod, too (good thing it's a big 20 GB model—each book was about 50 MB). I listened whenever I had a free minute.

Most programs on Audible.com are available in more than one size and quality. The bigger the file the better it will sound. I always chose the highest quality offered, 'cause my ears aren't as good as they used to be and I have lots of hard disks at home, so disk space is never an issue for me.

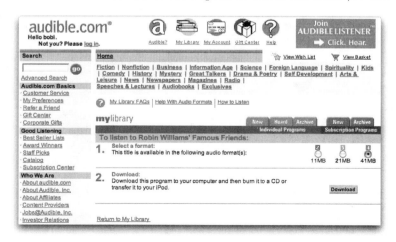

Your mileage may vary but the 11 MB version sounded thin and "tinny" to my old ears.

I've never been an audio-book fan but I have to admit this was pretty cool. Over the course of a week I heard two books I probably wouldn't have had time to read. That's a good thing.

Alas, the Robin Williams program, on the other hand, was kind of a gyp. Sure it was funny in spots—it's Robin Williams, for heaven's sake—but I expected more laughs and more content for my $20.

If you like spoken-word audio, check it out at www.audible.com.

All this is great for finding music to add to your Library. But sometimes, it's all too much trouble and you just want somebody else to spin the tunes while you work on your Mac. Fortunately, there's Internet radio…as you're about to discover in the next exciting chapter.

Internet Radio

There are thousands of Internet radio stations that "netcast" music (and talk) 24 hours a day, 7 days a week, over the Internet, and iTunes lets you listen to many of them.

The only catch to listening to Internet radio with iTunes is that the station must netcast streaming MP3 format (not the Windows Media Player or RealAudio formats).

Fortunately for us iTunes fans, tens of thousands do.

Netcast (also webcast, streaming, e-broadcast, and similar forms): Like a broadcast, but it's delivered over the Internet, rather than the airwaves. A netcast can include audio, video, or both. Often, netcasts are live feeds in real time.

Radio, Radio

Internet radio stations run the gamut from ragged underground and hard-core punk to FM station simulcasts and slicker-than-FM-radio professional products. Internet radio is mostly commercial-free, which is nice. And with so many stations, you can try something new and completely different or listen to the biggest hits. No matter what kind of music you enjoy, I'm pretty sure you'll find Internet radio stations that play it.

The built-in iTunes radio tuner includes almost 300 Internet radio stations, categorized and preinstalled for your convenience.

They're hard to count, as some of them appear in multiple categories (for example, the RTN Radio station appears in both the "70s Pop" and the "Classic Rock" categories). And some stations are provided at more than one bit rate (for example, the Super 70s station is available in 128, 56, and 24 kbps versions).

And for the most part, they're pretty darn good. No matter what you like to listen to when you sit at your computer—1950s and '60s pop, country, new age, classical, comedy, hip-hop/rap, soul, jazz, world music, hard rock/metal, or whatever—you'll find plenty to listen to among those built-in stations.

But wait, there's more. There's something even better than listening to those (perfectly fine) built-in Internet radio stations: You can add other stations. There are thousands upon thousands of these, and the best part is that some of those stations are demonstrably better than the built-in ones. (I'll even demonstrate just that a little later in this chapter.)

But first, let's take a look at the built-in stations.

Listening to built-in stations

Listening to an Internet radio station couldn't be easier. First, connect to the Internet if you aren't already connected. Now click Radio in the Source list, choose the type of music you want to hear, and click the triangle to the left of its name. The stations in that category appear, as shown in **Figure 9.1.**

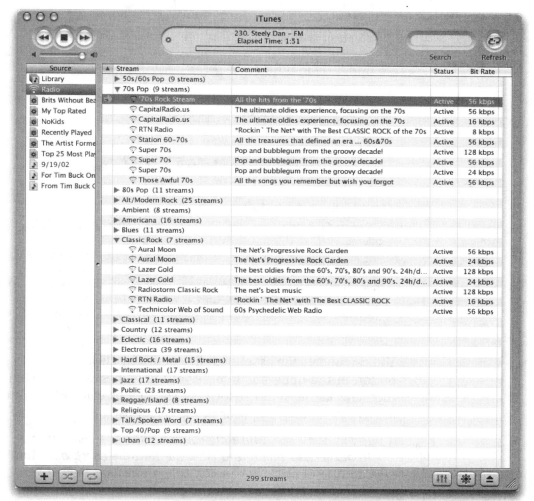

Figure 9.1 If I want to hear some '70s music, or classic rock I have at least a dozen choices.

I'm listening to the built-in station 70s Rock Stream. I've heard songs by Supertramp, Steely Dan, Talking Heads, Led Zeppelin, and the Doobie Brothers in the past half-hour. So it's at least as good as my local FM classic-rock station.

Just double-click a station to listen to it. After a few seconds, the music (or talking) will begin.

If you can't read all the text in the Comment column, you can make the column wide enough to read by dragging the dividing line to the right of the Comment column header (to the left of the word Status *here; notice that the cursor turns into a column resizer when it's over the dividing line).*

A Bit about Bit Rates

When Radio is selected in the Source list, the Detail list has a Bit Rate column.

The higher the bit rate, the better the sound quality; the better the sound quality, the more bandwidth you need. So if you use a dial-up modem to connect to the Internet, you want to choose a station with a bit rate of less than 56 kbps; if you have faster Internet service (such as a cable modem or DSL), you can handle the higher bit rates.

You can update the list of built-in stations by clicking the Refresh button in the upper-right corner of the iTunes window. iTunes then checks the Internet for new stations or categories; if any are available, they'll appear in the Detail list.

If you don't see a Bit Rate column, choose View Options from the Edit menu and click the Bit Rate check box. You can also Control-click in any column header, then choose the Bit Rate column from the pop-up contextual menu.

Last, but not least: You can't record or save songs from Internet radio.

But you can add stations to your Library or a playlist for easy access—just drag the name of each station you want from the Detail list into your Library or playlist.

Those built-in stations should keep you busy for a while. But remember when I said there was something even better than the built-in stations? Well, check this out.

Live365.com—even better Internet radio

There's a Web site called Live365.com (www.live365.com) that has thousands upon thousands of stations.

What a great idea this site is. It's organized by genre and searchable by keyword, so you'll have no trouble finding stations to sample. If you like, you can even create your own streaming MP3 radio station.

> *Unfortunately, the tool that makes it easier to make your own station is Windows-only. Boo. Hiss. Mac users can still do it, but it's more tedious.*

Give it a try: Open your Web browser and go to www.live365.com. Browse the categories until you find a station that seems interesting. Click the station's name to see details about it, as shown in **Figure 9.2.** Finally, click the speaker icon above the word Play to listen to the station.

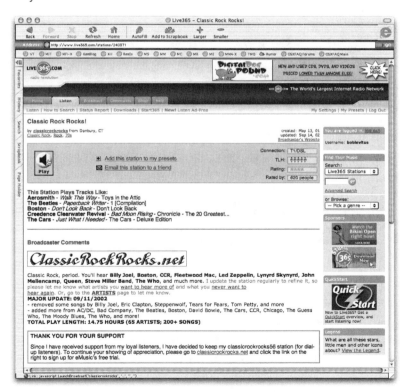

Figure 9.2 This station plays classic rock, which looks good to me, so I clicked the speaker icon.

After you click the speaker icon, iTunes will launch automatically (if it isn't already running), and the station will begin to play.

If that didn't happen when you clicked, your browser isn't properly configured. But don't worry, the instructions provided by Live365.com are excellent—just click the Help tab at the top of the page. Best of all, you'll only have to do it this once; once you've configured your browser, it'll work properly forever.

I saved the best part for last—the reason I say Live365.com is demonstrably better than the built-in stations. Here it is: After you click the speaker icon, your browser displays a small Player Window (see **Figure 9.3**) that shows you the title of the current song and the two previous songs. Hooray!

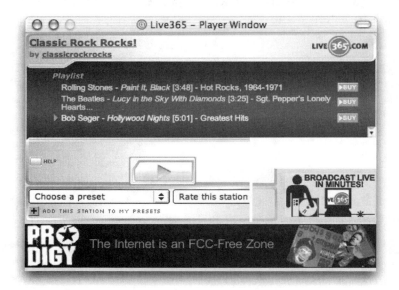

Figure 9.3 The Player Window tells you what you're listening to. It's way cool!

Does that rock or what? If you've ever been listening to the radio and desperately wanted to know a song's name, you'll love the Player Window. It solves that dilemma once and for all. In fact, I keep it visible while I work, as you can see in **Figure 9.4,** so I never have to wonder who sang that song or what its title is. Let's see your built-in stations do that!

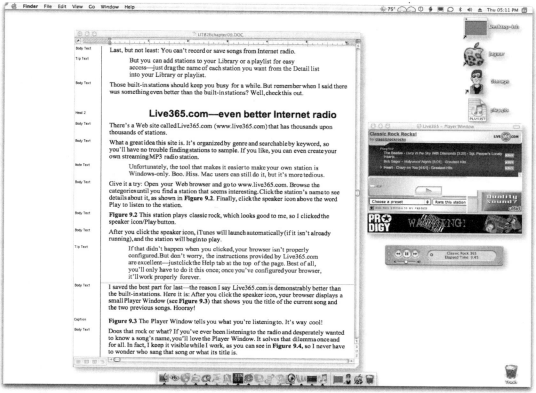

Figure 9.4 iTunes and the Live365.com Player Window keep me happy all day long (and often well into the night).

There is one thing about Live365.com that I don't like: The station appears in your Library after you click the Play button, but as you can see, its name is goofy.

Song Name	Artist	Time
☑ Tell Her No	Zombies	
☑ Time of the Season	Zombies	
◁)) ☑ ?SaneID=24.93.38.180-9880399...		Contin

So if you like a station from Live365, change its name to something meaningful before you forget. If, on the other hand, you don't like a station, just select it and press Delete (or Backspace) and—poof—it's gone!

Live365.com is by far the best site for streaming radio I've found so far. And, believe me, I've looked at a lot of Internet radio sites lately.

Still more Internet radio (if you need it)

If you aren't satiated with Internet radio by this time, there are still plenty more Internet radio stations out there for you to explore. Try this: Use your favorite search engine to search for words like *MP3, streaming,* and *Internet radio.* (Don't forget about www.mamma.com, "The Mother of All Search Engines.") You'll find plenty of stations to keep you busy.

Of course, not all of the results will be MP3 broadcasts, even if you include "MP3" as a search term. Still, if you're persistent, you'll certainly find plenty of stations this way.

If you already know the address

Last, but not least, if you know the URL for an MP3 stream, you don't need to use a Web browser at all. Just choose Open Stream from the Advanced menu (or use the keyboard shortcut Command-U), then type or paste in the URL and click OK. That looks like this:

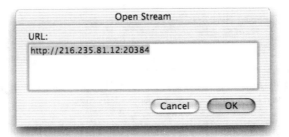

After a moment, the audio will start.

And that's all you need to know about Internet radio.

If you find an awesome station (surely you're familiar with my musical tastes by now), send me its URL!

In Chapter 10 you'll learn more about bit rates and sound quality, and their intimate relationship. You'll also be able to find out how sensitive your ears *really* are.

part four

More Stuff You Should Probably Know

Compression and Sound Quality

Now it's time to see how sensitive your ears are. Compression, as you remember, is the magic that makes CD audio files shrink when you rip them into MP3 files. The sound quality of the MP3 files relates directly to how much compression you use.

Compression is a good thing, but it involves a compromise: Your hard disk can hold up to 10 times as many songs, but the quality of the compressed songs is not as good as that of the original files. This is why, before you encode too many songs, I want you to have the opportunity to hear for yourself the effect of different amounts of compression. For your MP3 collection, you want to choose the compression setting that provides the best balance between file size and sound quality—for you.

Finding the best setting for you is what this chapter is all about. We'll start off with an overview of what compression does. Then I'll show you how to tinker with compression settings, reducing and increasing quality and file size. Finally, I'll give you a technique you can use to figure out how much compression sounds the best to your ears.

The Big Picture

As you know, an MP3 file is smaller than the uncompressed CD-DA or AIFF file from which you encoded it.

But as I mentioned way back in Chapter 1, MP3 uses a "lossy" compression scheme. That means some of the sound that was on the CD track isn't in the MP3 file—it's gone, and it's gone forever. So when you burn a CD using MP3 files you've encoded, even if all the songs are the same, the tracks are not exactly the same as on the original CDs.

Once you encode a song, you can't put back the stuff that compression removed.

Each person hears the effects of compression differently. Some people don't notice it at all, and may tell you that an uncompressed song and a heavily compressed song sound the same to them. Others with more discerning eardrums can wax rhapsodic for hours on the subtle differences between two similar compression settings.

You won't know how you feel about the matter until you try it. So first, I'm going to show you how to change compression settings so you can rip the same song several times at different bit rates (and different qualities). You'll end up with a playlist that looks something like **Figure 10.1.**

▲	Song Name	Bit Rate	Kind	Size
1	☑ Girlfriend—no compression	1411 kbps	AIFF ...	37.1 MB
2	☑ Girlfriend—(very low compression)	320 kbps	MPEG...	8.4 MB
3	☑ Girlfriend—(low compression)	192 kbps	MPEG...	5.1 MB
4	☑ Girlfriend—(medium compression)	128 kbps	MPEG...	3.4 MB
5	☑ Girlfriend—(high compression)	96 kbps	MPEG...	2.6 MB
6	☑ Thunder Road—no compression	1411 kbps	AIFF ...	48.6 MB
7	☑ Thunder Road—(very low compression)	320 kbps	MPEG...	11.1 MB
8	☑ Thunder Road—(low compression)	192 kbps	MPEG...	6.7 MB
9	☑ Thunder Road—(medium compression)	128 kbps	MPEG...	4.5 MB
10	☑ Thunder Road—(high compression)	96 kbps	MPEG...	3.4 MB
11	☑ Money—no compression	1411 kbps	AIFF ...	79.1 MB
12	☑ Money—(very low compression)	320 kbps	MPEG...	18 MB
13	☑ Money—(low compression)	192 kbps	MPEG...	10.8 MB
14	☑ Money—(medium compression)	128 kbps	MPEG...	7.2 MB
15	☑ Money—(high compression)	96 kbps	MPEG...	5.4 MB

Figure 10.1 This is my compression-testing playlist; notice the relationship between file size and bit rate.

You'll hear this again and again, but for the record: The higher the compression setting, the smaller the resulting file. So uncompressed files are huge but may sound better, while heavily compressed files are tiny but may sound worse.

After you rip all the songs at different bit rates, you'll want to burn a CD from that playlist. Listen to the CD to compare the quality of different compressions—try it first on your Mac with iTunes, and then elsewhere (your car, your home stereo, wherever). The whole process shouldn't take you more than an hour and the results may surprise you.

You could skip this chapter. If the thought of all this compression and file sizes and adjusting this and listening to that is giving you a headache, feel free to do just that—the iTunes default settings work fine.

On the other hand, if you skip this chapter, you'll never know: You could be wasting gobs of precious hard disk space, or amassing a collection of MP3 files that you'll later decide sound awful. If you skip the rest of the chapter you'll never know for sure.

Compress and Compress Some More

The first thing you need to know is how to change the bit rate for songs you rip. When you click the Import button in the main window or a playlist, iTunes uses the compression setting in the Preferences dialog box. So let's begin there.

Choosing a bit rate

1. First, choose Preferences from the iTunes menu to open the Preferences dialog box (keyboard shortcut Command-Y). Then click the Importing icon, as shown in **Figure 10.2.**

2. If "MP3 Encoder" is not selected in the Import Using pull-down menu, select it, since that's what we want to do—encode files using MP3 compression.

3. In the Configuration pull-down menu, choose "Good Quality (128 kbps)," then click OK.

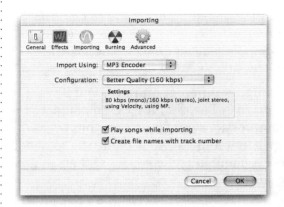

Figure 10.2
The Importing panel
of the Preferences
dialog box is where
you change the
bit rate

The iTunes default setting is "Better Quality (160 kbps)." So unless you've changed it, that's the setting your songs have been ripped at until now.

4. Insert the audio CD that contains the song you want to use for your compression testing.

Pick your song carefully. It should reflect the type of music you typically listen to and should sound good to you when you listen to it on a CD. Also, try to choose a song with both loud and soft passages, and clearly discernable instruments. (Of course, you can use more than one song if you wish, just keep these selection criteria in mind.)

5. Select the CD in the Source list and put a checkmark next to the song in the Detail list that you want to import.

When you first insert a CD, all the boxes are checked. Here's a shortcut to uncheck them all: Press the Command key while you click any check box. That will cause all the check boxes to turn on or off. (If that turned them all on, Command-click a second time.) Nice, huh?

6. Click the Import button and in a few moments the song will be added to your Library.

*It's a good idea to rename each song after you rip it, so you can see what it is at a glance. Rename this one "Song Title (128)." You'll also find it handy to put all the compression-testing songs in a single playlist, as I did in **Figure 10.1**. So create a playlist, name it "Testing Playlist," and drag this song into it.*

7. Now, repeat the whole process with the same song, but this time in Step 3 choose "Better Quality (160 kbps)." Rename this version "Song Title (160)" and drag it from the Library into your testing playlist.

In order to rip the same song at a different bit rate, you'll have to eject the CD and reinsert it. If you don't, iTunes will scold you and tell you to do it after you click the Import button. It seems silly, but that's how iTunes wants it done. (Why isn't there a "rip again" command?)

8. Finally, repeat the process with the same song, but this time in Step 3 choose "High Quality (192 kbps)." Rename this version "Song Title (192)" and drag it into your testing playlist.

That's it. You now have three versions of the same song in your testing playlist, each ripped at a different bit rate.

I know you're eager. And you could listen to them now. But I recommend you read the rest of the chapter first, as there's a bit (pun intended) more to it than meets the eye...er, ear.

Making a reference version

To test compressed songs properly, you should also hear them uncompressed, which will give you an accurate frame of reference.

Here's how to create that uncompressed AIFF version.

1. First, choose Preferences from the iTunes menu to open the Preferences dialog box (keyboard shortcut Command-Y). Then click the Importing icon, as shown in **Figure 10.2.**

2. Choose "AIFF Encoder" from the Import Using pull-down menu, since that's what we want to do— encode an uncompressed AIFF version of the file.

3. Choose "Automatic" from the Configuration menu and then click OK.

4. Insert the audio CD you used in the previous rips.

5. Select the CD in the Source list and put a checkmark next to the song in the Detail list that you want to import.

6. Click the Import button and in a few moments the song will be added to your Library.

7. Rename this one "Song Title (Uncompressed)" and drag it into your testing playlist.

That's it. You now have a fourth, uncompressed version of your test song in your testing playlist.

Choosing a custom bit rate

Three of the most common bit rates for MP3 files are 128 kbps, 160 kbps, and 192 kbps, which also happen to be iTunes's preset bit rates (Good, Better, and High Quality, respectively). But what if you want to use even more (or less) compression?

No problem—there are additional bit rates available in iTunes, if you know where to look for them.

1. First, choose Preferences from the iTunes menu to open the Preferences dialog box (keyboard shortcut Command-Y). Then click the Importing icon, as shown in **Figure 10.2.**

2. If "MP3 Encoder" is not selected in the Import Using pull-down menu, select it, since we want to encode a file using MP3 compression.

3. Choose "Custom" from the Configuration menu.

4. The MP3 Encoder dialog box appears. Click the Stereo pop-up menu, choose a new bit rate (as shown in **Figure 10.3**), and click OK.

5. Click OK in the Preferences dialog box.

6. Insert the audio CD you used in the previous rips.

7. Click the CD in the Source list and put a checkmark next to the song in the Detail list that you want to import.

8. Click the Import button and in a few moments the song will be added to your Library.

If you're going to use a custom bit rate in your testing, I'd suggest 64 kbps (very compressed) and 320 kbps (hardly compressed). You probably wouldn't use these exaggerated settings when you actually rip MP3s for your listening enjoyment, but they will help you hear the difference between compression settings in your testing.

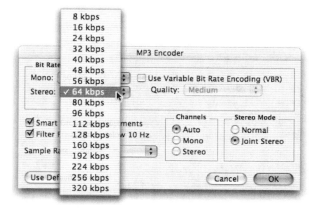

Figure 10.3
For those times when Good, Better, and High just aren't enough.

Digression on Custom Encoding

The MP3 Encoder dialog box has some other menus and check boxes that may affect both file size and sound quality. Since they're not covered elsewhere in the book, we'll take a quick look at them before we proceed.

Bit Rate: Rather than just accepting the canned bit-rate choices iTunes offers (Good, Better, and High Quality), this section of the dialog box lets you specify your own.

Mono and Stereo pop-up menus: These allow you to choose separate bit rates for monophonic and stereophonic recordings.

Use Variable Bit Rate Encoding (VBR) check box: VBR attempts to apply compression intelligently to different parts of the song. In theory, the parts of the song with a lot of audio information are compressed less, and the parts of the song with less audio information are compressed more. So a song encoded with VBR may be smaller and sound better than the same song encoded at a fixed bit rate. You couldn't prove it to me. First, I don't care that much about file size. Second, I don't hear much (if any) difference in quality between VBR and fixed-rate encoded files.

But the main reason I don't use or recommend VBR is that some (mostly older) MP3 players can't play files encoded with it. So for maximum file compatibility, don't enable VBR.

continues on next page

Smart Encoding Adjustments check box: If you enable this feature and the bit rate you've selected is less than 128 kbps, iTunes will eliminate the very highest frequencies (above 16 kHz—which most people can't hear anyway). This lets it preserve more of the middle frequencies (which most people can hear). Smart Encoding Adjustments have no effect when encoding at 128 kbps and higher.

Some people believe files ripped with Smart Encoding Adjustments enabled sound better.

Filter Frequencies Below 10 Hz check box: As with the very highest frequencies, most people can't hear very low frequencies. (And most speakers and headphones can't reproduce them anyway.) Use this option to tell iTunes to filter them out and, as with Smart Encoding, use the saved space to preserve the middle frequencies.

Some people believe files ripped with Filter Frequencies Below 10 Hz enabled sound better.

Sample Rate pop-up menu: Like bit rate, sample rate affects both the size and the quality of your MP3. Technically, "sample rate" refers to the number of times per second the audio signal is converted to digits, or "sampled." The higher the number, the more faithfully the digital sound recreates the original; but higher numbers also mean bigger file sizes (audio CDs are sampled at 44.1 kHz, and 22 kHz is roughly equivalent to AM radio). If you're ripping songs originally recorded at low quality (like transfers from 78 RPM records), use this setting to save disk space. The Auto setting maintains the sample rate of the source.

Channels; Auto, Mono, and Stereo radio buttons: Choose Stereo to rip stereophonic (two-channel) MP3 files; choose Mono to rip monophonic (single-channel) MP3 files.

Mono files are roughly half the size of stereo files. If you plan to listen to music on your Mac's solitary built-in speaker (on single-speaker Macs), stereo files are a waste of disk space. But if you *ever* plan to listen to these files on stereo speakers, you should probably choose Stereo or Auto here. In fact, Auto is probably the best choice—it rips monaural tracks into mono MP3 files, and rips stereo files into stereo MP3 files.

Stereo Mode; Normal and Joint Stereo radio buttons: In Normal mode, your MP3 file contains right and left stereo channels. Often, the two channels contain related information. Joint Stereo tries to intelligently store only information that differs between the two channels.

Your file won't be a true stereo file, but you probably won't be able to tell the difference. Some people believe files ripped with Joint Stereo sound better than ones ripped with Normal.

Use Default Settings button: Click this to revert to the built-in settings.

The last thing to do before you begin the actual testing is to burn a test CD.

If you've ripped more songs than a blank CD will hold, you'll want to delete some songs from your playlist before you click Burn CD.

My testing playlist looked like **Figure 10.4.**

#	Song	Bit Rate	Kind	Size	Time	Artist
1	Girlfriend—no compression	1411 kbps	AIFF ...	37.1 MB	3:40	Matthew Sweet
2	Girlfriend—(very low compression)	320 kbps	MPEG...	8.4 MB	3:40	Matthew Sweet
3	Girlfriend—(low compression)	192 kbps	MPEG...	5.1 MB	3:40	Matthew Sweet
4	Girlfriend—(medium compression)	128 kbps	MPEG...	3.4 MB	3:40	Matthew Sweet
5	Thunder Road—no compression	1411 kbps	AIFF ...	48.6 MB	4:48	Bruce Springsteen
6	Thunder Road—(very low compression)	320 kbps	MPEG...	11.1 MB	4:48	Bruce Springsteen
7	Thunder Road—(low compression)	192 kbps	MPEG...	6.7 MB	4:48	Bruce Springsteen
8	Thunder Road—(medium compression)	128 kbps	MPEG...	4.5 MB	4:48	Bruce Springsteen
9	Thunder Road—(high compression)	96 kbps	MPEG...	3.4 MB	4:49	Bruce Springsteen
10	Money—no compression	1411 kbps	AIFF ...	79.1 MB	7:50	Pink Floyd
11	Money—(very low compression)	320 kbps	MPEG...	18 MB	7:50	Pink Floyd
12	Money—(low compression)	192 kbps	MPEG...	10.8 MB	7:50	Pink Floyd
13	Money—(medium compression)	128 kbps	MPEG...	7.2 MB	7:50	Pink Floyd
14	Money—(high compression)	96 kbps	MPEG...	5.4 MB	7:50	Pink Floyd

14 songs, 1:17:51 total time, 248.1 MB

Figure 10.4 This set of test tracks just fits on an 80-minute blank CD.

*Actually, there's one last thing you should do before testing, and that is to create a label or list for your CD, so you can tell what you're listening to. The easiest way is to use the handy trick I taught you in Chapter 6. You should end up with something like **Figure 10.5.***

Figure 10.5 The label I created for my test CD, based on a screen shot of the playlist shown in Figure 10.4.

The Proof Is in the Hearing

Before you begin testing, think about what you're trying to do. The point of the exercise is to determine the bit rate that best serves your needs. So you're going to have to listen very closely to all the tracks, then determine whether and how much the differences between them bother you.

But what, exactly, should you be listening for? To my ears, uncompressed tracks sound "brighter"—the highs are crisp and shimmery and the lows are tight and clean. Cymbals sizzle and the kick drum has presence. Heavily compressed tracks, on the other hand, sound "muddy" to me—the highs are more subdued and the lows are duller.

Again, the differences are subtle. More than that, they depend a lot on the audio system you're using. If you're using an eMac and listening on its built-in speakers, you may not notice any differences at all—no compression and heavy compression may sound exactly the same. The same is true for many car stereo systems.

On the other hand, if you have an excellent home stereo system, a good set of amplified computer speakers (with a subwoofer), or a killer car stereo, you should hear a significant difference between compressed and uncompressed tracks. With all that in mind, let's do some listening!

You'll be hearing more about speakers (pun intended) in Chapter 12.

Testing 1, 2, 3

Start by comparing the uncompressed version with the most compressed. Listen to one, then immediately switch to the other. The difference between these two will be most apparent.

Next, compare the two compressed versions at either end of the spectrum—the ones with the lowest and highest bit rates. The difference will be more subtle.

Finally, compare two compressed versions with similar bit rates. The difference will be the most subtle of all.

Try this test in at least two different locations: on your Mac (using iTunes) and on your favorite CD player.

That's it! You are now ready to decide the best bit rate for *your* MP3 collection.

My conclusions

After completing this exercise myself, I concluded that Best Quality (192 kbps) and Better Quality (160 kbps) both sound darn good to me. In my car I couldn't discern much difference (if any) between 160 kbps and 192 kbps, or even between 160 kbps and uncompressed. But on my home stereo (which is better), I could hear definite differences, even between 160 kbps and 192 kbps. On the same system, I couldn't hear much difference (if any) between 192 kbps and 320 kbps.

So I made the decision to rip all my MP3s at either 160 kbps or 192 kbps from today forward. Though songs ripped at 192 kbps use more disk space than songs ripped at lower bit rates, I consider it a fair trade for the improved sound quality I hear.

In the next chapter you'll see how you *can* take it with you, as we explore the wonderful world of portable gadgets for listening to your MP3s.

Portable MP3 Players

11

Even though iTunes runs on a computer, you *can* take your MP3 tunes with you. There's the expensive way, with an iBook or a PowerBook, but there's also a cheap and convenient way—with a portable MP3 player.

Download MP3 files from your computer into one of these small, relatively inexpensive, battery-operated devices, and you can listen to your music anywhere. Though portable MP3 players aren't exactly cheap, they aren't particularly expensive anymore, either. And though a personal CD player may be less expensive than even the cheapest portable MP3 player, MP3 players have several distinct advantages, including size, storage capacity, and skip-free performance.

And most of them, especially the iPod, are cooler-looking than any CD player you've ever seen.

In this chapter we'll look at these handy devices—what they do, how they work, what features to look for when you shop for one, and how to use one with iTunes (it's so easy you'll laugh). Last but not least, we'll take a brief look at Apple's iPod.

Which happens to be, at least in my humble opinion, the greatest MP3 player ever made.

What to Look for in a Portable MP3 Player

Portable MP3 players come in a wide variety of sizes and shapes and offer a wide variety of features. Most are small enough to clip onto your belt, such as the tiny 2.4-ounce Rio 600 in **Figure 11.1** and the 2.7-ounce Nike-branded psa[play120 in **Figure 11.2.**

Figure 11.2 The Nike psa[play120 is another stylish little MP3 player made by Rio.

Figure 11.1 The Rio was one of the first portable MP3 players and is still among the most popular.

You think those two are small? Samsung has a line of wearable MP3 players half the size—dubbed "Yepp," shown in **Figure 11.3.**

Figure 11.3 The 1.13-ounce Mini Yepp (left) and 1.2-ounce Pendant Yepp (right) are among the smallest MP3 players on the market today.

These MP3 players achieve their diminutive size by using ultra-small and lightweight (but expensive) solid-state flash memory to store your MP3 files. Alas, they can only hold a few hours of music.

Other portable MP3 players forgo the expensive flash memory, so they're bigger but they're also capable of storing much more music at a much lower cost per megabyte. For example, the Nomad Jukebox shown in **Figure 11.4** weighs 14 ounces and uses a 20 or 40 GB hard drive that holds 600 hours of music or more.

The RioVolt shown in **Figure 11.5** also eschews expensive flash memory, but instead of a hard drive, it uses CD-ROMs to hold your MP3 files and can also play standard audio CDs.

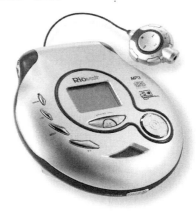

Figure 11.4 The Nomad Jukebox by Creative Technology can store up to 600 hours of music on its 40 GB hard disk.

Figure 11.5 The RioVolt is a dual-function music player—it can play regular audio CDs, but it can also play 20 hours or more of MP3 files from a CD-ROM.

Most portable MP3 players include these features:

- USB connection
- headphones
- battery operation
- storage (for 1 hour to thousands of hours of music)
- basic audio controls—volume, next/previous track, tone
- basic display (track number)

Prices range from less than $100 to more than $500. The more you pay, the more songs your MP3 player will hold, and the more features it will have.

I'll go into a bit more detail about memory in the next section. Meanwhile, these are some optional features to look for in your MP3 player:

- expandable storage
- changeable faceplates
- equalizers
- expanded display (song title, artist, volume level, and so on)
- playlist-management capability
- ability to play audio CDs in addition to MP3 files
- recording/dictation
- can be used as a hard disk in addition to playing MP3s
- FireWire instead of or in addition to USB

How Portable MP3 Players Store Files

In the previous section I touched on the different kinds of memory that portable MP3 players use to store your songs. Since the amount of music it holds may well be the most important consideration in choosing your player, let's take a closer look.

You'll find three basic types of storage used in MP3 players: solid-state (flash memory), magnetic (hard disk), and optical (CD-ROM). Each has its pros and cons.

Solid-state memory is tiny but very expensive. For example, the Rio 600 with 64 MB of memory—enough for 1 or 2 hours of MP3 music—costs more than $125, and an additional 32 MB "backpack" costs an additional $40. So for just under $200 you can have roughly 4 hours of tunes.

On the other hand, an MP3 player that uses a hard disk for storage is a much bigger device, but provides far more storage for your money. For example, the Nomad Jukebox costs around $400 with a 20 GB hard disk that can hold more than 100 hours of music. But it's eight times the size of the teeny, tiny, solid-state players like the Rio or psa[play120.

Players such as the RioVolt that store your MP3 files on a CD-ROM are also larger, less expensive, and hold more music than the solid-state players. For example, the RioVolt costs around $150 and can store roughly 20 hours of music on a single CD. Additional blank CDs, as you know, cost less than $1. An added advantage with this type of player is that they can also play audio CDs. But they're big—roughly the same size as an ordinary personal CD player.

Last, but not least, I should warn you that the amount of music each type of device will hold is approximate—your mileage may (and probably will) vary.

Of course, you can always fit more tunes on your device by ripping them at a lower bit rate. (Though, as you learned in the last chapter, you'll sacrifice some sound quality if you do.)

Using a Portable MP3 Player with iTunes

Using a portable MP3 player with iTunes is easy. But first, I have to inform you that as of the day I wrote this iTunes supports only a handful of portable MP3 players other than the iPod: Sonic-blue's Rio, RioVolt, and Nike psa[play (www.sonicblue.com); Creative Technology's Nomad series (www.nomadworld.com); and the Nakamichi SoundSpace 2 (www.nakamichi.com).

The SoundSpace 2 is way, way cool. It's an AM/FM stereo radio, alarm clock, speaker system with subwoofer, dictation machine, and (this is the coolest part) a detachable, 3-ounce MP3 player and recorder. The whole shebang weighs less than 2 pounds, runs on battery or AC power, and has a remote control. It's the ultimate boom box and an MP3 player/recorder. At $500, I can't justify buying one. But that doesn't mean I wouldn't love to have it. Go check it out at the Nakamichi Web site.

Don't despair. Apple will no doubt add to that list over time, so visit the Apple Web site before you go shopping.

If you do decide on an MP3 player that isn't supported by iTunes, don't worry: As long as the player supports the Macintosh, you'll be able to use it. You'll have to use software other than iTunes to download songs to it, but you *can* use your iTunes MP3 files. It's a trifle inconvenient, but if the MP3 player that really rings your chimes isn't supported by iTunes (but does support the Macintosh), it's certainly worth considering.

Having said that, I can save you a lot of time (but not money): Buy the iPod. Nothing else comes close. I've owned them all— Rios, Nomads, RioVolts, and more—but since the day I got my first iPod, I haven't used anything else.

I'm on my third iPod, a 20 GB model. Whenever Apple introduces a bigger and better model, I hand down the old and buy the new. My wife and daughter are the happy beneficiaries.

How to download songs to a supported MP3 player

Fire up iTunes, and plug your MP3 player into an available USB port. A playlist for your MP3 player will appear in the Source list. Drag songs into it—when the MP3 player's memory is full, it'll tell you. That's it.

I told you it was so easy you'd laugh.

This section is short for a reason: You absolutely must read the manual that came with your player. I can't do this one for you—each player works differently with iTunes and I only have one player here. Sure, I could tell you how my (now discontinued) Rio 500 works (if I could even find it around here today), but unless you also happen to have one, what I told you would probably be totally wrong.

Furthermore, if your player happens to support optional features such as multiple playlists, the manual is where you'll find instructions for using them, not this book. So I beg of you: Read the instructions that came with your MP3 player to find out how to use it with your Mac. You'll be glad you did.

How to download songs to an iPod

If you thought the previous section was easy, wait until you see this one. Fire up iTunes and plug your iPod into an available FireWire port. (Is this starting to sound familiar?) OK. You're done. Really. Within a few minutes (depending on the number of songs), iTunes will politely inform you that the update is complete.

Unless you've changed one of the iPod preferences (more on that in the next section) iTunes will launch automatically if it isn't already running, and then automatically transfer your Library's contents to the iPod, all without human intervention.

iPod quick configuration

If you want to change what happens when you connect the 'Pod to the 'puter, open the iPod preferences dialog box by clicking the little iPod icon next to the Equalizer button.

The iPod Preferences dialog box appears:

The top half of the window determines what happens when your iPod is connected to your Mac:

- **Automatically update all songs and playlists** copies every song in your Library to your iPod.

- **Automatically update selected playlists only** copies every song on every playlist with a checkmark next to its name to your iPod.

- **Manually manage songs and playlists** copies no songs or playlists to your iPod.

If you choose the last item you can still put songs or playlists in your iPod by dragging them onto the iPod icon in the Source list.

The three check boxes in the bottom half of the window offer additional options for your iPod:

- **Open iTunes when attached** does what it sounds like it would do—determines whether iTunes launches automatically when it detects your iPod connected to a FireWire port.

- **Enable FireWire disk use** allows the iPod to mount its hard disk in the Finder. You can then copy files to it and use any available space (i.e., space not used by songs) to store regular old Macintosh files and folders.

*I copied an OS 9 System Folder, a folder full of OS 9 disk and file utilities, my contact list, and my calendar to my iPod's hard disk, as shown in **Figure 11.6**.*

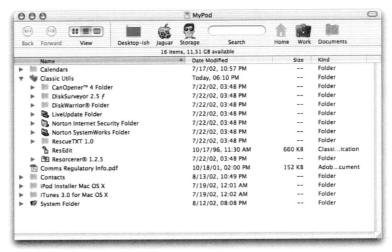

Figure 11.6 My iPod acts as a bootable repair and maintenance disk if necessary.

This allows me to use my iPod as a boot disk for most Macs manufactured in the past 5 years and perform repairs if needed. Since I carry the 'Pod with me everywhere I go, I've saved more than one Mac from a trip to the repair shop.

If you're wondering where my 6.5 GB of music are, the iPod renders them invisible. Why? To remind you not to not steal (or give away) music. That said, within days of the iPod's release dozens of little freeware utilities appeared that allow you to turn them visible again and drag them hither and yon, just like ordinary Mac files (which is what they are, even if they are invisible at times).

- **Only update checked songs** gives you finer control over what gets copied to the iPod—rather than every song in the Library or every song in your selected playlists, only songs that have a checkmark next to their names will be copied to the iPod regardless of your choices in the top half of the Preferences dialog box.

I could go on and on about the iPod I love mine so much. I'd write a book about it, but my old Mac User *"Help Folder" co-writer, Chris Breen, beat me to it. His* Secrets of the iPod *(from this very publisher—imagine that!) is chock-full of tips, hints, and techniques. Since the iPod (like iTunes) comes with almost no documentation, if you want to get the most out of it, this little gem is highly recommended.*

Portable MP3 players—and especially the iPod—are nifty indeed, but they aren't the only sweet temptations for MP3 fans. If you love iTunes, there's still a bunch of other cool stuff you may enjoy. Not surprisingly, that's what the next chapter is called—"Other Cool Stuff."

So limber up your wallet and read on.

Other Cool Stuff

12

If you like iTunes, there are some software and hardware products that you may also enjoy, such as speakers, hard drives, CD-RW drives, and remote controls (yes, a remote control for iTunes!). Every product I describe in this chapter makes iTunes better.

At least they make it better in my opinion. I've been using iTunes since the day it came out (and before that I used its predecessor, SoundJam MP), so I've had a lot of time to evaluate the things I claim make it better. Furthermore, I've extensively tested every product I discuss and give each of them my highest recommendation.

So let's take a look at some cool stuff.

Hardware

Hardware isn't cheap—some of the products in this section cost hundreds of dollars. But every one of them is worth considering if, like me, you use iTunes all day every day. The joy these products have brought me far outweighs the pain I felt when I wrote the check.

So do what I do: Don't consider these items an expense, consider them an investment in your eternal auditory happiness.

Speakers

Even though Macs have better speakers than other PCs, their speakers still suck. Apple definitely tries harder, but in my humble opinion there's never been a Mac with decent speakers, and there probably never will be.

That's why Apple makes it so easy to add a set of speakers to a Mac. Unlike other PC users, we Mac folk don't need no stinkin' sound cards to connect speakers to our computers!

Most Macs include a standard minijack speaker connector, but some models (most notably the G4 Cube) don't. For those models you'll need speakers that connect with USB. So I'll recommend one set of each type.

Look for speakers specifically designed for use with a computer. Computer speaker systems (sometimes known as "multimedia speakers") have two distinct advantages over plain old stereo speakers. First, they're "shielded," which means their magnets won't mess up your monitor, even if you place the speakers right next to it. Second, they're "powered," which means that they have a built-in amplifier. That's necessary because your Mac's own audio amplifier, though better than that of most other PCs, is still pretty wimpy.

You should also look for a three-piece speaker system that includes a subwoofer. Without a subwoofer, the low end of the sound spectrum (the "lows" or "bass") will sound thin and tinny; on a speaker system with a subwoofer, those bass notes will rattle your innards (I mean that in a good way).

If you like computer games, speakers make them better, too! I love the sound of a dwarf exploding (in Myth I, II, or III) or a rocket liquefying an enemy (in Quake 3 Arena, Unreal Tournament, or actually just about any first-person shooter) on my three-piece speaker system.

You can find computer speaker systems with subwoofers for well under $100. And some of them are pretty good. Still, both of the speaker systems I like and recommend cost a bit more.

My favorite speakers—the ones I use every day—are the flat-panel Sonigistix Monsoon iM700s in **Figure 12.1.**

Figure 12.1 My favorite speakers are these Monsoon iM700s.

The big, square box in the middle is the subwoofer.

Monsoon iM700s (and, indeed, all of the Monsoon models) offer amazing spatial imaging, incredible clarity, and accurate sound positioning. My system includes a built-in 44-watt amplifier, a subwoofer, the two flat "planar focus" speakers, connection cables, and a totally wonderful little volume-control "puck" that sits on my desk. The whole shebang sells for around $170.

What I like best is that you can crank these suckers way, way up, without any distortion whatsoever. They're easily the loudest, cleanest-sounding computer speakers I've tried.

They aren't cheap but they're worth every penny. I've used at least a dozen different speaker systems with my Mac over the years (and reviewed many of them in newspapers and magazines), and the Monsoon iM700s are the best so far.

The Monsoon iM700s connect to your Mac with a standard audio minijack.

My second-favorite speaker system is perhaps the most beautiful set of speakers ever made for a computer—Harman/Kardon's SoundSticks shown in **Figure 12.2.**

Figure 12.2 Harman/Kardon's SoundSticks: absolutely gorgeous.

The SoundSticks' spatial imaging, clarity, and sound positioning are all very good, but not nearly as good (to my ears) as that of the iM700s. Also, the SoundSticks sound better when you're sitting in front of your computer with both speakers pointed directly at your ears; if you move away from this position, they don't sound nearly as fine.

The Monsoons, on the other hand, sound great regardless of where you sit or stand.

The SoundSticks include a built-in 30-watt amplifier, a subwoofer, the two speakers, and connection cables, and cost around $200. If style is your thing, these are the speakers you want.

The SoundSticks connect to your Mac with USB.

Alas, though the SoundSticks sound great and look even better, the Monsoon iM700s sound noticeably better at high volumes. And I miss the handy volume-control puck—you get one with the Monsoons but not with the SoundSticks.

Unless you only use iTunes to burn CDs, you absolutely need a good set of speakers.

Headphones may suit your needs better than speakers, and many Macs also include a headphone jack. Even if yours doesn't, Radio Shack sells plug converters that will let you connect headphones to the speaker minijack. And headphones may be less expensive than speakers, as well.

External CD-RW drive

I touched on third-party CD-RW drives briefly in Chapter 2, but let's revisit the topic for a moment. If your Mac didn't come with a built-in CD-RW drive, an external model that iTunes supports is just the ticket.

Once again, that list of supported drives can be found at www.apple.com/itunes/compatibility.

I've tried three external FireWire drives so far—one made by LaCie, the Que Fire drive I talked about in Chapter 2, and a FirewireDirect 48X Turbo CD-RW (see **Figure 12.3**).

Figure 12.3 I'm quite happy with this speedy Turbo CD-RW drive from FirewireDirect.

The LaCie drive is a 16 x 10 x 40 FireWire/USB drive that cost around $340 in early 2001.

But, as happens with most consumer electronics products, that model has been discontinued, replaced by a faster drive that costs less. Today you can buy a LaCie 48 x 12 x 48 with FireWire and USB for about $220.

The same is true of the Que drive. Mine is an 8 x 4 x 32 FireWire drive that cost around $280 a year ago. Today a faster 24 x 10 x 40 FireWire drive from Que is about $180. (Assuming the company stays in business.)

The FirewireDirect drive, my latest acquisition, is a 48 x 12 x 48 they sell direct for around $190.

Those numbers (16 x 10 x 40, 48 x 12 x 48, 8 x 4 x 32, and so on) refer to CD-R recording speed, CD-RW recording speed, and CD-ROM playing speed, respectively.

The LaCie was twice as fast and had both FireWire and USB, so I could use it with my G4 as well as with my older iMac and iBook, which don't have FireWire. But the LaCie had a major flaw, at least for me—its fan was loud enough to hear from the next room!

The Que drive was slower and didn't include a USB connector (though it did include a nifty vinyl carrying case), but it was significantly less expensive and virtually silent.

The FirewireDirect drive is the fastest and cost me the least, but I bought it a year after the Que and LaCie. It's fast, quiet, and priced attractively.

All of the drives were simple to set up and easy to use; all three drives worked flawlessly throughout my testing. But when all was said and done, even though the LaCie was faster and had USB, I preferred the quieter, less-expensive Que drive, which was then replaced by the quiet and inexpensive (but much faster) FirewireDirect drive.

A great big external hard disk

It's a fact: Although MP3 files are compressed, they still use up a lot of hard disk space. The more MP3s you have, the more storage space you're going to need. And though you can burn CDs or CD-RWs to store your music files, having an additional hard disk connected to your Mac all the time is much more convenient.

External hard drives connect to your Mac with USB (slower but a little less expensive) or FireWire (faster and slightly more expensive). They're plug-and-play, so you just connect them and they're ready to use.

Sizes vary and prices fluctuate so widely I'm not going to even try to quote them here. And there are so many brands I haven't tried that I can't really recommend one over another. Still, I had to at least mention them in this chapter.

Keyspan Digital Media Remote

The Keyspan Digital Media Remote (DMR) is the nifty little gadget shown in **Figure 12.4.** It lets you control multimedia applications—including iTunes—from across the room. After you install the included software that makes the magic happen, just point the tiny keypad at the base unit connected to your Mac.

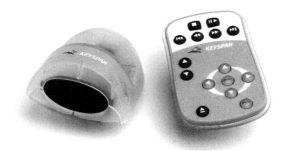

Figure 12.4
The Keyspan Digital Media Remote is way cool.

It's really quite ingenious for a $50 software/hardware combo. The tiny wireless keypad talks to the DMR base unit using infrared. The DMR base unit connects to your Mac with USB. The magic is coordinated by special software that translates the infrared signals from the keypad into the keystrokes you normally use to control the application from the keyboard. For example, if your program uses the N key to advance to a new slide, the DMR can send the same keystroke to your application when you press the Forward key on the keypad. Better still, it comes preprogrammed to work with iTunes, so it's plug-and-play. Best of all, at about $50, it's affordable.

The DMR also works great with PowerPoint, QuickTime, DVD players, CD players, and other MP3 players.

PowerMate

Griffin Technology's PowerMate is a volume knob and much, much more.

Figure 12.5 The PowerMate's base glows and pulses with gorgeous blue light that's simply beautiful to behold.

PowerMate, of course, acts as a master volume control for your Mac, but it includes software that lets you configure it for use with iMovie (jog/shuttle controller), a Web browser (scroll wheel), or just about anything you can conceive of in any just about any application.

It's made of high-quality machined aluminum and feels like an oversized volume knob on a world-class stereo system. Its heavy weight and precise feel are nothing like most cheap plastic USB peripherals.

Highly recommended if only because it looks so cool.

Multimedia keyboard

Out of all the hardware toys I've mentioned, the one I find most useful with iTunes is the Microsoft Natural Keyboard Pro, shown in **Figure 12.6.**

*The Natural Keyboard Pro has a row of buttons above the function keys that control iTunes even when it's not the active application or when it's hidden. I **love** that!*

If the phone rings, I press the Mute button. If the song playing isn't one I want to hear, I press the Next Track button. I can play, pause, stop, increase or decrease the volume, and more, all without moving my fingers more than a few inches. I keep trying other keyboards but this one has the features I keep coming back for.

Figure 12.6
The row of buttons above the function keys can control iTunes.

And, it's the best keyboard I've tried for real work (typing), too.

Last but not least, it includes excellent software (shown in **Figure 12.7**) that lets you assign and reassign any multimedia key to any function in any program. So the multimedia buttons can perform different functions when you're using iMovie, iDVD, Microsoft Office, or any other program.

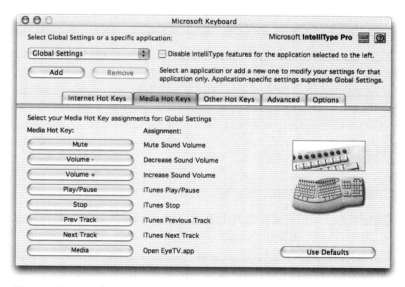

Figure 12.7 Make any button do anything you like in any program.

Software

There are plenty of programs out there that can help you do all kinds of things with your MP3s: programs that let you find files on the Internet, edit the music inside MP3 files, change file attributes of MP3 files, and even burn better-sounding CDs. I've discovered three great programs that enhance iTunes in various ways. Each does something incredibly useful, and so is worth at least knowing about.

Two of the programs are shareware; I downloaded both from my favorite downloadable software repository, the VersionTracker Web site (www.versiontracker.com).

MP3 Rage

MP3 Rage (see **Figure 12.8**) is a regular Swiss army knife for working with MP3 files. Its developer, Chaotic Software, calls it "the ultimate MP3 tool," and I'd have to agree.

Here are just some of the things it can do:

- Search for and download MP3s and other files from the Internet using the Gnutella or other file-sharing systems.
- Export MP3 files as AIFF, WAV, QuickTime Movie, and AVI for CD burning and distribution.
- Organize your MP3 files (or create aliases to them) by genre, artist, album, and so on.
- Rename your MP3 files based on their tag info (song title, for example).
- Create a catalog of your MP3 files using tag info (for input into a database, for example).
- Find MP3 files in your collection using tag information.
- Change file attributes for batches of files.

Just one example of how I've used MP3 Rage, was to change the attributes of a folder full of MP3 files I had created with SoundJam MP before iTunes came out. When I double-clicked any of them, SoundJam would launch, but I didn't want that to happen anymore once I got iTunes. So I used MP3 Rage to change the whole folder from files that launch SoundJam into files that launch iTunes.

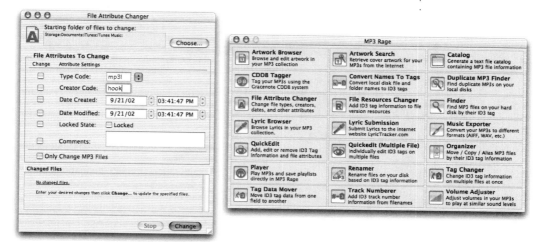

Figure 12.8 MP3 Rage can do a lot, including change creator code and file type to the ones used by iTunes ("hook" and "mp3!" respectively).

MP3 Rage is simple to use: Just drag MP3 files (or folders full of MP3 files) onto the application or its windows, select the options you want, and click a button. That's it.

MP3 Rage is shareware. You can try it before you pay, but if you continue to use it, you're honor-bound to send $24.95 to Chaotic Software.

Amadeus II

Amadeus II (see **Figure 12.9**) is a useful tool that allows you to process, generate, and analyze MP3 audio files. It has many powerful functions, among them the ability to apply audio effects such as echo or pitch shifting to a song.

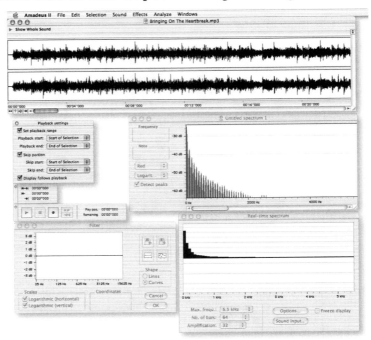

Figure 12.9 Yeah, Amadeus II is complicated, but it does things no other program I know of can do.

One of its best features is its ability to edit songs, cutting out pieces you don't want or combining pieces of two songs into one. It also offers several file-repair functions, which you may find helpful if you encounter a damaged MP3 file. Finally, for you experienced audiophiles out there, it includes a variety of analysis tools I don't really understand yet.

Amadeus II is a bit complicated, doesn't have the slickest interface (as you can see), and has little documentation. But it can do a lot of useful massaging to your MP3 files. So I firmly believe that it's worth downloading and taking for a spin.

Amadeus II is shareware. You can try it before you pay, but if you continue to use it, you're honor-bound to send $25 to the developer, Martin Hairer.

Toast 5 Titanium

If you have a CD-RW (or recordable DVD) drive, you'll love Toast 5 Titanium. According to its developer, Roxio, Toast is "the most powerful CD recording software ever developed for the Macintosh." I have to agree wholeheartedly: If you burn CDs (or DVDs), you'll find that Toast makes it easy to create, organize, share, and store all of your digital content on either CD or DVD.

Of course, iTunes can also burn audio CDs. But if you're serious about CD recording, you'll want a copy of Toast anyway, for all the other great things it can do. Here are just a few of them:

- Create data, audio, multimedia, video, and hybrid CDs or DVDs.
- Burn data CDs in the background while you continue working on your computer.
- Convert iMovies into video CDs that are playable on most DVD players.
- Turn MP3 files into standard audio CDs or burn them onto MP3 discs.
- Convert any analog source (LPs, cassettes, even live music) into CDs and clean up your old recordings by filtering out unwanted noise, hisses, and pops.
- Organize, sort, and store digital photos and multimedia files on CDs.
- Design and print your own custom CD labels, covers, and inserts.
- Burn CDs simultaneously on multiple CD recorders.

Toast has a fabulous, uncluttered, easy-to-use interface, as you can see in **Figure 12.10.** And it makes extensive use of drag-and-drop. So, for example, to duplicate an existing CD, you just drag the audio CD's icon onto Toast's main window.

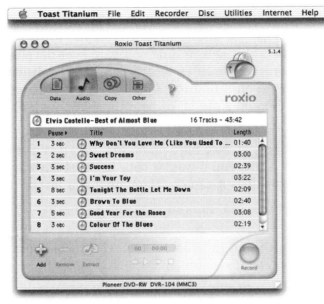

Figure 12.10 Toast is easy to use, but extremely powerful.

You can even delete songs you don't care for before you burn your duplicate, a feature I think is quite nifty.

Duplicating a CD with Toast has a hidden advantage: The duplicate CD may sound better than if you had made it with iTunes. That's because Toast doesn't automatically rip the files into MP3s before converting them back to CD-DA for burning. The default behavior for iTunes is to encode the files as MP3s (Good Quality, 160 kbps), and that is what it will do unless you've selected the AIFF encoder before encoding. Toast is also demonstrably faster at burning CDs than iTunes.

Making data CDs is just as easy—simply drag files or folders onto Toast, then click the Record button.

Some other high points include the ability to burn QuickTime movies onto video CDs, which can be played on PCs (Mac or Windows) as well as on many consumer DVD players.

This is very cool. It means you can make video discs that people can watch with a DVD player and television without investing in an Apple SuperDrive (CD/CD-RW/DVD-R combo).

Another nice touch is the included Magic Mouse Discus label-printing program, which lets you make beautiful, artistic-looking CD labels and jewel box inserts like the one in **Figure 12.11**.

Figure 12.11
The templates and painting tools included with Toast make it easy to create gorgeous labels for your CDs.

I can easily say that you aren't getting the most out of your CD-RW drive if you aren't using Toast.

Toast 5 Titanium is commercial software that sells for around $100.

And that, gentle reader, is the end of my story—I hope you had as much fun reading it as I had writing it. And please feel free to drop me a line sometime. Let me know what you liked, and even what you didn't like about this book. And in the unlikely event you find a mistake, please let me know so I can fix it in the next edition. Send everything to LITB2E@boblevitus.com.

Thanks.

iTunes System Requirements and Installation

This short appendix includes the system requirements for iTunes and how to install the program. It's short, sweet, and painless.

System Requirements

Here are the official iTunes 3 system requirements (annotated by yours truly).

Hardware

According to Apple, these are the hardware requirements for iTunes 3:

- Macintosh with built-in USB ports
- 400 MHz G3 processor or better recommended
- 256 MB RAM recommended
- Supported CD-RW drive required to create audio CDs

But as I said way back in Chapter 2, when Apple says other models aren't supported, it doesn't mean that iTunes won't work on them; it just means don't come crying to Apple for help. In fact, iTunes works just fine on many older Mac models, even some that lack such modern frippery as USB ports.

System software

iTunes 3 works with Mac OS 10.1.4 or later, but OS 10.2 ("Jaguar") or later is highly recommended. If you're using Mac OS 9 you're out of luck, at least as far as iTunes 3 goes. But iTunes 2 worked just fine with Mac OS 9.1 and later (9.2.1 highly recommended), so if you can find a copy, you're good to go; if not, you'll need to upgrade to Mac OS X to use iTunes.

Search Apple's support site for iTunes 2. Though Apple doesn't draw attention to it, older versions of Apple software can often be found on the Web site in the Support section. I'd provide the URL but they often change and the current one is too long for most people to type accurately.

OK, if you insist, here it is: http://a1408.g.akamai.net/5/1408/1388/e47e6bd4eaf34e/1a1 a1acd38990667d0fe67d53baad839a91985ea187bea5786ef43b 8268bfe305fd44776e344a7/iTunes_2.0.4_Installer.smi.bin.

Supported MP3 players

On the day I wrote this, iTunes supported the following players:

MP3 Players	Manufacturer	Format
iPod	Apple	FireWire
Nomad II	Creative Labs	USB
Nomad II MG	Creative Labs	USB
Nomad II c	Creative Labs	USB
Nomad Jukebox	Creative Labs	USB
Nomad Jukebox 20 GB	Creative Labs	USB
Nomad Jukebox C	Creative Labs	USB
Rio One	Sonicblue/S3	USB
Rio 500	Sonicblue/S3	USB
Rio 600	Sonicblue/S3	USB
Rio 800	Sonicblue/S3	USB
Rio 900	Sonicblue/S3	USB
psa]play 60	Sonicblue/S3	USB
psa]play 120	Sonicblue/S3	USB
SoundSpace 2	Nakamichi	USB
RioVolt SP250	Sonicblue/S3	
RioVolt SP100	Sonicblue/S3	
RioVolt SP90	Sonicblue/S3	

This list isn't gospel, it's just the current list of supported MP3 players from Apple's iTunes page at www.apple.com/itunes. So if you're considering an MP3 player that isn't on the list, check to see if it has been added since I wrote this.

Supported CD-RW drives

For a current list of supported drives, please visit www.apple.com/itunes/compatibility.

That's the fourth and last time I'm going to say that in this book!

Installing iTunes

Begin by launching the iTunes installer (iTunes3.pkg). You'll be asked to provide your name and password or phrase. Do so and then click OK.

The "Introduction: Welcome to the iTunes for Mac OS X Installer" screen appears. Read it and then click the Continue button.

The "Read Me: Important Information" screen appears. Read it and then click the Continue button.

You can click the Print or Save button first, if you want to print or save the Read Me information.

The "Select a Destination" screen appears. Click your boot disk at the top of the window to select it and then click the Continue button.

The "Easy Install" screen appears. Click the Install button. A dialog box will warn that installing this software requires you to restart your Mac when the installation is done. Click Continue Installation to install iTunes 3 on your boot disk; click the Cancel button to return to the "Easy Install" screen.

The iTunes program will be installed in your boot disk's Applications folder. When the installation is complete, a dialog box will suggest that you restart your Mac, as shown in **Figure A.1.** You probably should.

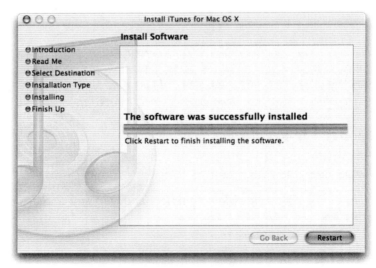

Figure A.1 You don't have to do it this very second but you'll need to click the Restart button before you can use iTunes 3.

iTunes Setup Assistant

The first time you launch iTunes after installation, the iTunes Setup Assistant appears to (what else?) help you set up iTunes. It'll ask you some questions; you'll make some choices that will configure iTunes properly for your needs. Here's how it goes:

The first screen welcomes you to iTunes. No action is necessary yet, so just click the Next button to proceed.

The "Internet Audio" screen shown in **Figure A.2** appears. You need to answer its questions before you move on.

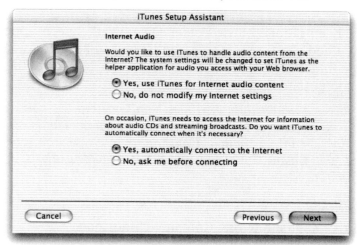

Figure A.2 Click a radio button for each of the two questions, then click the Next button.

The first question asks how you want to handle MP3 audio streams from the Internet. If you click the Yes button, iTunes will launch automatically whenever you encounter an MP3 stream with your Web browser. If you click the No button, whatever program is currently set to handle MP3 streams will continue to handle them.

My preference is Yes.

The second question asks whether or not iTunes should check with you before it connects to the Internet to look up song titles and artists from CDDB. If you have a dial-up connection, I recommend clicking No. If your Internet connection is "always on" (cable modem, DSL, and the like), I recommend clicking Yes.

After you click a radio button for each question, click the Next button.

The "Find MP3 Files" screen appears. It offers to find any MP3 files you have on your hard disk and add them to your Library.

I strongly recommend you choose No. If you choose Yes, you may be surprised when you see all the unfamiliar MP3 files iTunes finds and adds to your Library, including sounds from long-forgotten games, sounds from movies or animations, and lots of other junk that you probably don't want in there.

The "Keep iTunes Music Folder Organized" screen appears. Read it and choose Yes if you want iTunes to keep your iTunes Music folder organized, or No if you prefer to change the file and folder names yourself.

This is a new feature in iTunes 3 and one that's a blessing. I vote in favor of clicking the "Yes, I'll keep my iTunes Music folder organized" button. I can't think of any reason you wouldn't want iTunes to perform this monkey work for you, but it's your call.

Click the Done button and…you're done.

And that's all she wrote. Go enjoy iTunes now….

How to Back Up Your Music (and Should You Bother?)

This appendix deals with a pair of issues: how to back up your music library, and whether backing it up is even necessary.

There are only two kinds of Mac users: those who have lost data, and those who are going to. If you don't back up your work, you will lose valuable data. Period. Your novel. Your Quicken files containing the last three years of checking-account activity. Your Accounts Receivable files. Or even (gasp!) your entire collection of MP3s.

I'm a firm believer in backing up your important data, but I'm not sure you absolutely have to back up your MP3 files. So in this appendix we'll begin with a brief discussion of whether you even need to back up your MP3 collection, followed by a short section on how to back up.

This appendix is short, sweet, and well worth reading. If you choose not to read it, don't come crying to me when you lose all your music.

Should I Back Up My MP3s?

Should you back up your MP3 files? The answer is a definite maybe. While I absolutely believe you should back up important data, backing up your MP3s is more of a personal preference. The more MP3 files you have, the more thought you should give to whether or not to back them up.

If you only have a handful of MP3s, it's a no-brainer—just do it. Include them in your regular data backups (see the next section). Or burn them onto a CD, copy them to a Zip or Jaz disk, or copy them to your iDisk, and you're done with it. But if you have thousands of MP3 files, the time it will take you and the cost of backup media may become significant. So backing up your MP3s may or may not be a worthwhile pursuit to you.

Here are some other things to consider:

- If you have every song in your MP3 library on audio CD as well, backing up is a convenience, not a necessity. If you should experience a disaster and lose the contents of your hard disk, you could re-rip all the songs at your convenience and have all your music back in a few hours (or days, depending on the size of your collection).

- On the other hand, if you have a lot of MP3 files you've obtained in any way other than burning them from your own CDs (downloaded, received from friends, and so forth), they can't easily be replaced and you probably should back them up.

- How much time and money is your MP3 collection worth to you? The bigger your collection, the more time and money it will take to back it up. Is it worth it? That's a question only you can answer.

- Do you care? If all your MP3s were gone tomorrow, would you be heartbroken? Or would you not care at all? The answer to this question should really be the determining factor in whether or not you bother backing 'em up.

So there you have it. You now have sufficient information to make this important decision for yourself. If you've decided you don't need to back your MP3s up, you're done—you can skip the rest of this appendix.

If, on the other hand, you've decided you *should* back up your MP3s, here are some observations and recommendations about how to do it.

How to Back Up

If you already back up other data on your hard disk regularly, all you need to do is make sure the iTunes Music folder is included in your regularly scheduled backups. That's it. You don't even need to read the rest of this section.

If you aren't backing up your data regularly, first let me say that you absolutely and positively should be. While hard disks are generally quite reliable, there's no question that some day yours will fail. I'll say it again. There are only two kinds of Mac users: those who have lost data, and those who are going to.

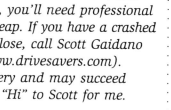

If you do experience a hard disk crash—and believe me, one day you will—and you don't have a backup, there is still a chance you will be able to recover your files. If you're handy with Norton Utilities, have at it. If that doesn't work and the data is really important to you, you'll need professional help. Though I warn you, it isn't cheap. If you have a crashed disk with data you can't afford to lose, call Scott Gaidano at DriveSavers (415) 883-4232 (www.drivesavers.com). DriveSavers is expert at data recovery and may succeed even after others fail. Oh, and say "Hi" to Scott for me.

OK. Now that that's out of the way, let's talk about how to actually do it. You can back up in two ways—manually or the easy way.

Manual backups

One way to back up your files is to do it manually. That means dragging files you want backed up onto removable media such as Zip or Jaz disks, or using your CD-RW drive to burn your files onto a CD.

This method sucks. It takes a long time, you never know if you've copied all the important stuff, and there's no easy way to copy only files that have been modified since your last backup.

Of course, if all you want to do is back up your iTunes Music folder, this method may be all you need. But, if you want to back up properly (and painlessly), you will need a good backup program.

The easy way: use Retrospect

Retrospect, from Dantz Development (www.dantz.com), is by far the best Mac backup solution. It completely automates backing up, remembering what is on each backup disk (if your backup uses more than one disk) and backing up only files that have been modified since your last backup.

Better still, you can instruct Retrospect to ignore stuff that doesn't need to be backed up, such as applications, system software, or anything else that you can easily reinstall from its original CD-ROM. Or you can set Retrospect to back up only a single folder, if that's what you want.

Furthermore, Retrospect works with just about any type of media—Zip, Jaz, CD-R, CD-RW, Orb, magneto-optical disks, or tape. So you can almost certainly use it to back up files to a storage device you already own.

A copy of Retrospect Express will set you back around $70, but it's money well spent.

Index

X

XML (extensible markup language), 97–99

Y

Yepp MP3 players, 158

Z

.zip files, 10
Zip utility, 10
Zoom button, 34
Zoom command, 108